AN ECC

AN ECONOMIC HISTORY OF GHANA FROM THE EARLIEST TIMES

FRANCIS AGBODEKA
Formerly Professor of History Universities of Cape Coast, Ghana and Benin, Nigeria

GHANA UNIVERSITIES PRESS
ACCRA
1992

Published by
Ghana Universities Press
P. O. Box 4219
Accra.

© Francis Agbodeka 1992
ISBN 9964—3—0198—7

PRODUCED IN GHANA
Typeset by Ghana Universities Press, Accra
Printed by Assemblies of God Literature Centre, Ltd., Accra

CONTENTS

List of Tables ... ix
List of Figures ... ix
Preface ... xi

Chapter
1. **Economic Prehistory** ... 1
   The Geographical Setting ... 1
   Neolithic Revolution ... 1
   Economic and Technical Setbacks ... 5
   Earliest Traces of Man in Ghana ... 5
   Ghana's Early Economy ... 6
   Notes ... 7

2. **The Gold Era** ... 9
   Factors of Economic Growth ... 9
   Origins of Gold Mining and Trade ... 9
   The Expanding Trade ... 12
   Results of the Expanding Trade ... 14
   The Rise of Crafts, Extractive and Manufacturing Industries ... 15
   Iron Extraction and Mongery ... 15
   Gold Mining and Smithery ... 16
   Pottery ... 17
   Cloth Making ... 17
   Salt Making ... 18
   Woodworks ... 19
   Minor Industries ... 20
   Rapid Development in Agriculture ... 21
   Notes ... 22

3. **The Slave Era** ... 25
   Origins of the Atlantic Slave Trade ... 25
   Expansion of the Slave Trade ... 26
   Trade Routes ... 31
   Decline of Arts and Crafts, Extractive, Manufacturing and Agricultural Industries ... 33
   General Results of the Slave Trade ... 35
   Notes ... 36

4. **The Oil Palm Era** 37
   General 37
   Origins and Early Development of Oil Palm 37
   The 19th Century Agricultural Setting 38
   The Role of Oil Palm Industry 40
   Decline of the Oil Palm Industry 41
   Cotton 41
   Rubber 43
   Coffee 45
   Trade 46
     Local and International Trade 46
     Roads 47
     Trade Routes 47
   Transportation 50
   Crafts, Extractive and Manufacturing Industries 52
   Notes 54

5. **The Cocoa Era** 56
   Political-economic Situation 56
   Origins of Cocoa Industry 56
   The Spread of Cocoa Cultivation 57
   Effects of Cocoa Industry 60
   Cocoa Diseases 65
   Notes 68

6. **The Cocoa Era: Agriculture** 71
   Improved Techniques 71
   Diversification 73
   Agriculture Department and Problems of
      Agriculture 74
   Failure of Agricultural Cooperatives 79
   State Farms 79
   Export Crop Production 81
     Oil Palm 81
     Rubber 83
     Cotton 84
     Coconut 86
     Citrus 87
     Coffee 88
     Bananas 88
   Food Crop Production and Livestock Development 88

	Food crop	88
	Livestock	91
	Fishing	92
	Forestry – timber	96
	Notes	99
7.	***Towards a New Era: Mining, Communications Trade and Commerce, Finance***	105
	General	105
	Mining	105
	Gold	106
	Diamonds	110
	Manganese	113
	Bauxite	113
	Communications	116
	Trade and Commerce	123
	Finance	127
	Notes	129
8.	***Towards a New Era: Industrialization***	134
	General	134
	Industrialization in the Pre-1950 Period	134
	Industrialization in the 1950s and 1960s	141
	Notes	149
9.	***Towards a New Era: Trends and Prospects***	152
	General	152
	Industrialization	152
	Agriculture	152
	Mining	158
	Construction	158
	Foreign Trade and Finance	160
	Since 1983	161
	Notes	163
	Possible Examination Questions	165
	Bibliography	173
	Index	179

LIST OF TABLES

Table 1	Diamond Production and Export Value, 1942–46	112
Table 2	Comparative Figures of Mineral Production during the War, 1939–45	115
Table 3	Comparative Figure for 1947–48, 1948–49 Mineral Production and Value	116
Table 4	Private Cars and Taxis Imported into Ghana by 31st December, 1939	120
Table 5	Value of Export of Selected Domestic Goods, 1951–62 As Per cent of Total Exports	124
Table 6	Sources for Financing the Ghana 10-Year Development Plan, 1951–61	146

LIST OF FIGURES

Fig. 1	Ghana: Physical Features	2
Fig. 2	Ghana: Natural Vegetation	3
Fig. 3	Ghana: Trade Routes in the 19th Century	48
Fig. 4	Fall of Cocoa Producer Prices 1927–30	63
Fig. 5	Ghana: Agricultural Production	90
Fig. 6	Gold Coast and Asante Road Network 1906	118
Fig. 7	Ghana: Mineral Production and Railways	122
Fig. 8	Comparative Value of Ghana Chief Exports in 1958, 1975 and 1981	159

PREFACE

African History, as a discipline, is now established in most schools and colleges throughout black Africa and elsewhere. But so far, it is Political History that dominates the curriculum and attracts most research funding and scholastic attention in nearly all institutions.

Political History is not only more dramatic than Economic and Social History but also more rewarding in terms of research findings. Early African nationalist activities, a major contributor to the rise of African History, were geared to increasing political power of the activists. They believed that full sovereignty could be achieved only through the exercise of political independence to promote economic development. Some dissatisfaction was expressed at the slow rate of economic development under the Colonial Administration, but by and large the nationalist agitation concentrated on political freedom as a gateway to economic emancipation. Their attitude was summed up in Kwame Nkrumah's injunction "Seek ye first the political kingdom and all other things shall be added unto you".

The belief then was that, as colonialism was the perpetrator of multinational companies, the economy of Third World countries would continue to be exploited by multinational companies until these countries shook off the colonial yoke. It was then not clear that neo-colonialism would replace colonialism and help to entrench multinational activities in politically-independent states. In Africa, therefore, it is not surprising that it was largely the continent's political history that received attention since the late 1940s.

Political independence came but "all other things" were not added. The expectant populace failed to reach the promised land flowing with milk and honey. The academics among them, through the mass media and regular publications, began to ask what went wrong. These discussions have nearly always touched upon economic and social questions but it has still not been found necessary to expose more pupils and students in educational institutions to a comprehensive study of the events that have brought some Third World countries to the brink of disaster. Political History of Africa still dominates the scene at the expense of Economic and Social History. Economic History of Africa, of West Africa, of Ghana etc., has not featured, as much as it should, in the curricula of schools and colleges and there is hardly any awareness as to how the pitfalls of the past can be avoided in future.

Part of the problem is the lack of suitable resource material for teaching African Economic History. A few detailed studies of rather limited aspects of African Economic History exist, such as those on minerals, trade etc., but there are no comprehensive studies worth mentioning apart from Ralph Austen's book, *African Economic History,* published in 1987 by James Currey (London); and national economic histories are few and far between. In West Africa, for instance, apart from Hopkins' *Economic History of West Africa* (Longman 1973), Ekundare's *Economic History of Nigeria* (Methuen 1973) and to a lesser degree *Topics on Nigerian Economic and Social History* (ed. I. A. Akinjogbin and S. O. Osoba) published by University of Ife Press Ltd. Ile-Ife, there is not much of value suitable for a comprehensive study of West African economic histories. Ghana, in particular, is seriously handicapped in this respect, and until this is rectified, interest in Economic History of Ghana will be hard to awaken. It is hoped that the present work will, as it were, set the ball rolling.

The message that this work intends to put across is simply that from the 15th to the 17th centuries Ghana started on the road to economic prosperity but during the 19th and 20th centuries was thwarted by imperialism and colonialism. Weaknesses of the post-colonial economy are also examined and explained. The work is concluded with a discussion of trends and prospects of Ghana's economic future. The work is illustrated with over a dozen maps, tables and graphs.

The book is first and foremost directed to College and University students who may later enter the teaching profession and thus expose more students to the subject. Furthermore, the language used in the book is simple enough to make it particularly useful as a text-book for the second and third year Senior Secondary School history courses, and the general public should also find it both stimulating and educative.

In writing this book, I made extensive use of Annual Departmental Reports in Ghana, Despatches from Ghana to the Colonial Office and Parliamentary Debates which I consulted mainly in the Ghana National Archives in Accra and Cape Coast. I have also depended on articles in learned journals as well as secondary material in books.

The idea of writing an Economic History of Ghana first

dawned on me during the University of Cape Coast History Department seminars on Economic and Social History which I organized from 1974 to 1980. Apart from the views of my own departmental colleagues, I benefited from contributions of scholars in the other Social Science Departments of the University. The decision to definitely write the book came while I was on sabbatical leave from the University of Cape Coast in 1978, part of which I spent collecting relevant material from the Public Record Office, Kew Gardens, London. Most of the data for this work, however, has come from GNA whose staff both in Accra and Cape Coast I now wish to thank. I owe similar gratitude to the staff of the University of Cape Coast Library and Balme Library of the University of Ghana. While I was in the University of Benin, Nigeria, as Professor of History (1980–1986), I had access to research grant which enabled me to collect material, among other places, from the University Library, Ibadan. I found most of the Departmental Reports on Ghana Agriculture in Ibadan University Library and I am grateful for this opportunity, which I utilized primarily for research into Nigerian Economic History, the notes for which are still awaiting a write-up. During the planning stage of this work, I had interactions with History scholars both in the Department of History, University of Benin, and in the annual congresses of the Historical Society of Nigeria from 1980 to 1986. My thanks go to these Nigerian historians. From the Department of History University of Ghana, Dr. Albert Van Dantzig's comments on the introductory chapter helped me to clarify my own ideas on aspects of the work. In the same Department is Mr. Samuel N. Adumuah, whose clerical assistance made the final stages of this work possible.

Francis Agbodeka

Chapter 1

ECONOMIC PREHISTORY

The Geographical Setting
The story of Man's economic activities must begin with his surroundings which influence those activities. Ghana is part of tropical Africa which consists of a wide crescent of savannah, surrounding an evergreen forest. The tropical African rain forest favours root crops, and different types of cereals such as various forms of millet and rice, are said to be indigenous in the well-watered savannah areas.[1] Ghana shares most of these agricultural facilities with the rest of tropical Africa and was probably the home of another local species, the oil palm tree. It was well-watered land (*see* Fig 1) which favoured the growth of the vegetation cover, as shown in Fig. 2, which in turn promoted these rich agricultural faciles. The present total land area of the country is just under 2,600,000 square kilometres, rich in minerals and in a large variety of useful timber.

Neolithic Revolution
Neolithic revolution was an important milestone in the struggle of Man to harness the resources of Nature to his own advantage. This struggle was to ensure the survival of the human race and this decisive stage known as the neolithic revolution was reached in tropical Africa before the 13th century BC, although its major features were widespread only much later around 500 BC.[2]

The foremost characteristic of this neolithic revolution was regular food supply made possible by the replacement of hunting with the domestication of animals, and of food gathering with the cultivation of crops. Some scholars are chary of crediting tropical Africa with an independent invention of agriculture arguing that these ideas were imported from the Middle East.[3] However, Professor G. P. Murdock has shown that around 500 BC, agriculture was initiated, independently of South West Asia, in the Upper Niger area, by the ancestors of the Mande-speaking peoples. Besides, the well-proven existence of early pottery in tropical Africa is indicative not only of high technical ability of the people, but also of sedentry life which is the pre-condition for the emergence of agriculture.[4]

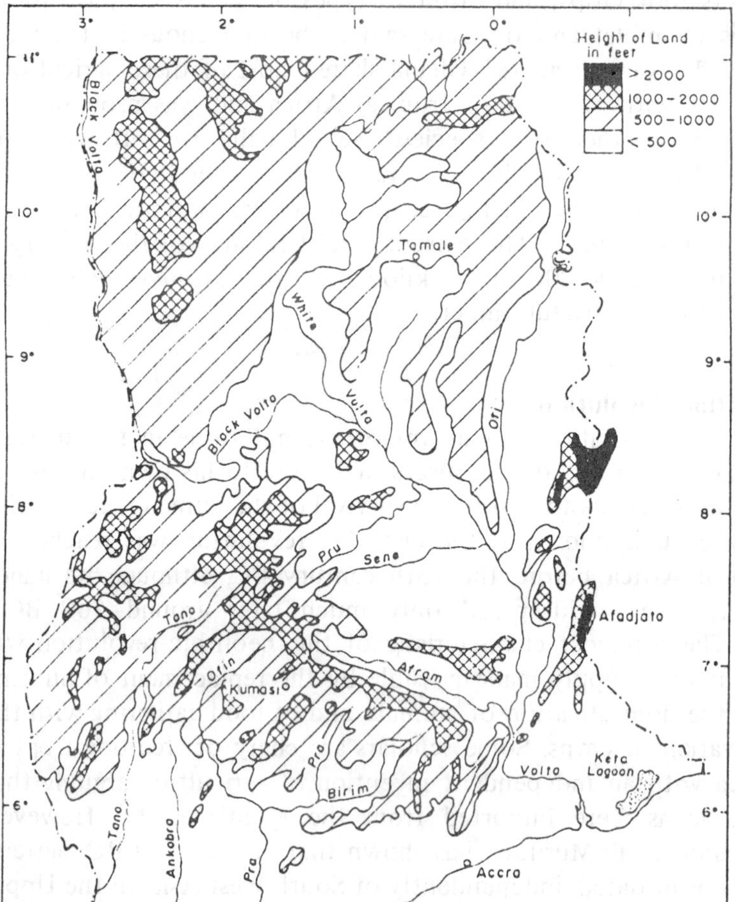

2   *An Economic History of Ghana*

Fig. 1   Ghana: Physical Features

Economic Prehistory 3

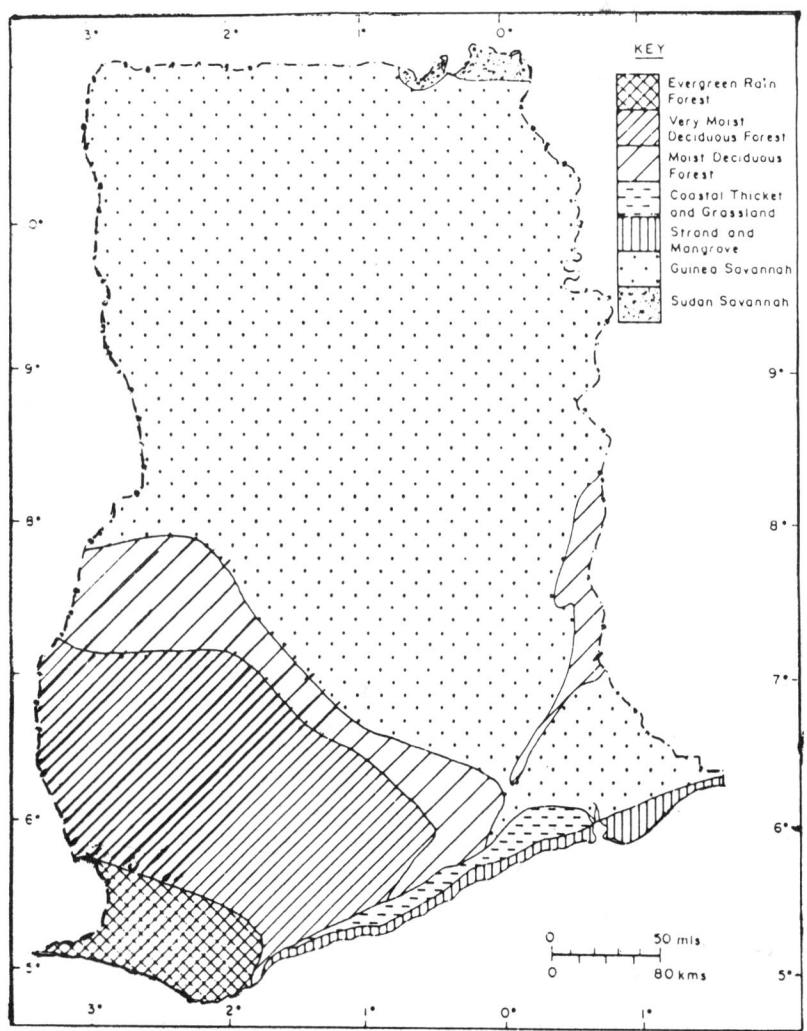

Based on D. T. Adams, *A Ghana Geography*, Fig. 47 p. 75

Fig. 2 Ghana: Natural Vegetation

A necessary feature of the neolithic period was the advance in tool making, without which agriculture could not have developed. Man's first attempt at tool manufacture is presumed to be the pre-Chellean pebble-tools. These were light and of limited use. The coming of heavy stone tools, therefore, represents an important step in human development.[5] In parts of West Africa including Ghana, the introduction of heavy stone axes and hoes featured prominently as part of the neolithic economy before 500 BC. Their use in the north of the wooded savannah of tropical Africa is believed to be as far back as 5000 BC when a digging culture using these heavy stone tools is known to be already penetrating the Nile Valley, and later the Upper Niger and Senegal basin.[6] It was much later, as already indicated, that these developments reached the forested south, where modern Ghana is situated.

A third feature of the neolithic period in tropical Africa was the types of crops cultivated with the tools invented at the time. A number of indigenous West African tubers were the first to be cultivated and this was of course before the arrival of Asian species. The local Hausa potato, for instance, preceded the imported cocoa yam. Shea butter and the oil palm are also indigenous.[7] Other indigenous crops of the forest zone are kola, rubber and coffee.[8]

The cultivation of the tubers probably began with the early digging of wild indigenous ones. We know of their cultivation in the Southern Sahara regions, watered by the Upper Niger and Senegal rivers. In these same regions, the cultivation of millet was introduced in the 4th millennium,[9] or, according to G. P. Murdock, who extended the list to Guinea corn, maize and rice, around 5000 BC.[10] The ancient province of yam culture, later noticeable over the whole forest and woodland zone of Africa must have been the extension of skills acquired during the Upper Niger and Senegal basin invention.[11]

Lastly, the domestication of animals was an important feature of the neolithic revolution in tropical Africa. Here, the ideas seem to have come from Egypt and Western Asia. The pre-neolithic Sebilian culture of Upper Egypt had produced, among other things, domesticators of cattle and it is almost certain that tropical Africa acquired its first stock from this source in the fifth millennium or earlier. Also there are suggestions that tropical Africa had contact with Western Asia in the matter of skills in the domestication of animals.[12] From about the 5th century BC, therefore, with the flowering of neolithic culture in tropical Africa, domestication of livestock including goats, sheep and cattle was being actively pursued by people on the savannah edge of the Niger basin, close to the tropical forests.[13]

Economic and Technical Setbacks

It was the existence of facilities in the agricultural sector such as fertile river basins, indigenous species of food crops and contact with the Mediterranean world that made domestication in tropical Africa possible, using the improved tools of the New Stone Age.[14]

During the domestication period, tropical Africa was almost at par with the North (i.e. Egypt, the Middle East and West Pakistan) in development. But during the next period of post-domestication expansion, economic development of tropical Africa suffered severe setbacks. In the first place, tropical Africa had no copper, the use of which or its alloy, bronze, ushered in the metal age in the North. Secondly, between the 1st millennium BC and 4th millennium BC, and more precisely by 1225 BC in places,[15] tropical Africa was entirely cut off from the North by the huge physical and climatic barrier created through the dessication of the now impassable Sahara. This meant that when North Africa and Eurasia moved from the stone age into the metal age by the 3rd millennium BC, West Africa continued with stone implements, and consequently missed the plough and the wheel. Without the plough, cultivation of large estates was impossible. Small peasant holdings, therefore, prevailed not allowing surplus food production for population increase or capital growth and economic specialization as was the case elsewhere. The absence of the wheel adversely affected transportation, so vital to the growth of an exchange economy.[16] These were serious drawbacks for West Africa and they were some of the factors that determined the course of Ghana's early economic history.

Earliest Traces of Man in Ghana

The story of Man in Ghana predates the neolithic period. Even though Man's first entry into Ghana was late compared with, say, the southern part of Africa, yet it was of fairly respectable antiquity, at least some 50,000 years ago,[17] having occurred not later than the Kageran-Kamasian Interpluvial and certainly before his appearance in Europe.[18] The evidence for this is in the pebble-tools of Yapei belonging to the Kageran Kamasian Interpluvial. There is probably a gap in cultural growth and Man seems to have moved away because of climatic conditions, but the next culture, the Chellean, that we find in the more definite and specialized forms of stone tools on the River Dayi in Togoland[19] indicates Man's return to Ghana. This was followed by another wave of invaders bearing the Sangoan culture. When subsequently Man left Ghana again, it was about 15,000 years ago that he once more returned, this time for good.[20]

All along, these early invaders of Ghana occupied only grassland and wooded savannah areas. Even much later when after 1300 BC stone hoe-users fled the dessicated Sahara and penetrated the south, they still avoided the forest areas until about 500 BC when they finally entered the true forest and made several clearings in what is now Asante.[21]

Most of the present inhabitants of Ghana are descendants of more recent immigrants who imposed themselves on the original occupants. Of the present population of Ghana only the Moshie and Dagomba peoples in the North have been there for a fairly long time. They must have been caught in the widespread net of Malian influence, now exhibited by their ruling families. The other sections of Ghana's present population came in from two directions. The Akan groups came from the north and reached their present abodes from 1300 AD onwards. The Ga and Ewe groups moved in from the east reaching their present homes not earlier than 1500 AD.

Ghana's Early Economy

The successive waves of immigrants into Ghana built so solidly on the ancient foundations of the original inhabitants that their culture remained in tact in spite of widespread Wangara influence in West Africa. This meant that, despite Ghana's technical drawback discussed above, a strong foundation was laid for economic development there.

Several factors made for rapid economic growth from about 500 BC onwards. First, the hoe-users whose southward movements reached a peak about 1300 BC were products of the neolithic revolution. They possessed improved stone implements for agriculture. Secondly, since they had been involved in domestication of plants and animals in their wooded savannah homelands, they possessed a vital knowledge for survival in their new surroundings in the south. Thirdly, they were a hardy people toughened by experiences of dessication. This was why in spite of the disadvantages of missing the bronze age, they turned their stone implements to cultivation in the forest, which began in earnest around 500 BC. The stone implements used for digging and clearing the forest were widespread in Ghana from south to north.[22] Lastly, from 300 BC, iron smelting techniques reached the Sudanic grasslands and a little later, the forest peoples acquired it and used it to expand their agricultural activities.

NOTES

1. Davies, O. 1960. The Neolithic revolution in tropical Africa. *Transactions of the Historical Society of Ghana iv (ii)*: 14—20.
2. *Ibid.*
3. Wrigley, Christopher 1960. Speculations on the economic pre-history of Africa. *Journal of African History 1 (2)*: 189—203.
4. *Ibid.*
5. Davies, O. 1961. *Archaeology in Ghana,* p.4, London: Thomas Nelson.
6. Davies, O. 1960. *Op. cit.*
7. *Ibid.*
8. La Anyane, S. 1963. *Ghana Agriculture, Its Economic Development from Early Times to the Middle of the Twentieth century,* p.8. London: Oxford University Press.
9. Davies, O. 1960. *Op. cit.*
10. Agbodeka, Francis 1986. *The Roots of Our Present Economic Woes,* 22nd Inaugural Lecture, University of Benin, Benin City, Nigeria. Unpublished.
11. Wrigley, Christopher 1960. *Op. cit.*
12. *Ibid.*
13. Agbodeka, Francis 1986. *Op. cit.*
14. Davies, O. 1960. *Op. cit.*
15. *Ibid.*
16. Agbodeka, Francis 1986. *Op. cit.*
17. Davies, O. 1958. Earliest man and how he reached Ghana. *Universitas* 3: 35—37.

18. *Ibid.*, Davies, O. 1961. *Op. cit.*
19. Davies, O. 1958. *Op. cit.*
20. *Ibid.*
21. Davies, O. 1960. *Op. cit.*
22. La Anyane, S. 1963. *Op. cit.*, p. 5.

Chapter 2

THE GOLD ERA

Factors of Economic Growth
The gap created in the early economic development of Ghana and, for that matter, in that of West Africa as a whole by the absence of copper, resulting in a low level of food production, population growth and economic specialization, could not be completely filled up with the coming of iron tools. These tools, coming after stone tools, did make some difference in Ghana's agriculture, but not enough to go beyond small peasant holdings to the characteristic large estate and relatively mechanized farming of the bronze age. So the country's agriculture, using crude methods, remained inefficient.

Nevertheless, what an inefficient agriculture could not do, international trade could, if commodities other than agricultural produce existed to promote it. Ghana has had one such commodity in the form of the king of metals – gold. Consequently, with the acquisition of skills in gold workings sometime after the 1st century AD., the country was set on the road to economic recovery from the ill effects of a weak agricultural framework. This period of rapid economic development terminates with the 17th century.

Origins of Gold Mining and Trade
The earliest period of gold mining and trade in Ghana is what we consider as the first important era in the development of Ghana because the activities involved did not just dominate the period economically but also set Ghana on the road to economic prosperity.

The people laying the foundations of this 'golden era' of Ghanaian history descended from the stone hoe-users who moved south around 1300 BC and entered the forest and auriferous regions of Ghana by 500 BC. As we have seen, these hoe-users were endowed with sterling qualities and it is, therefore, not surprising that their descendants should acquire the knowledge of iron workings just before the beginning of the Christian era and later that of gold, and thus provide this precious commodity for international trade.

Equally important was the existence of gold in Ghana. The

southern portion of the country west of the Volta was dominated by two geological formations known as Birrimian and Tarkwain Systems.[1] These systems stretched over a 240 kilometre zone from Tarkwa northwards through Bogosu, Prestea, Bibiani, Obuasi and Konongo.[2] Since ancient times, they have housed gold, either as lode ore in quartz reefs (Birrimian) or banket (conglomerate) reefs (Tarkwain).[3] Lode in quartz reefs is the richer ore, found mainly at Obuasi and banket is concentrated at Tarkwa.[4] The second source of gold is oxidized ores which are outcrops of the two gold bearing formations mentioned above. The third source of gold in Ghana has been alluvial deposits. Grains of gold existed loose and free in the gravels and sands of river beds, particularly in the Ankobra and Prah rivers, but also in the Offin and the Tano as well. The mineralization of this entire auriferous zone is put at some 2,200 million years ago.[5]

It has been categorically asserted that Akan gold-production provided a great stimulus to economic growth in Ghana before the arrival of Europeans.[6] We are not certain of the exact date of the acquisition of the skill in gold mining and workings in Ghana. A long period of quiet development in the pre-Akan period had resulted in the growth of peaceful economic activities like digging and collecting gold. When the Akans arrived, they improved upon gold mining and by the 16th century, the Akan region is known to have been producing some 1,380 kilogrammes of gold yearly.[7]

Long before the news of Ghana's gold reached the outside world, there had been going on internal trade in salt and gold. At the mouth of the little river Benya in Elmina, salt was extracted and traded north for gold in the Akan forest.[8] The art of gold smithery developed, and in Elmina and elsewhere, the wearing of heavy gold ornaments dates from very early times.[9]

Next came international trade with the north. A prosperous trade in gold, the origins of which lie in the 13th or 14th century, was established between the auriferous regions of Ghana and the great towns of the Niger Bend which formed the termini of the trans-Saharan caravan routes. The universal importance of gold dates back to a mystical past. In the Middle Ages, this importance was increasingly seen in its role as a stabilizer of national economies. Thus, in the early modern age, Western Europe acquired gold to meet the needs of its expanding money economy.[10] The principal source of gold was West Africa, whence it was brought across the Sahara through North African ports to Europe. The gold-bearing areas of the Western Sudan were the primary source. But the search further afield into the tropical forest was inevitable, particularly since the news of Akan gold trade and industry must have by now reached the outside world. A vigorous southern traffic grew and the growth of Jenne on the Niger Bend was specifically to control it. It was then that a southern imporium was founded for this traffic in the Banda country between the northern edge of the high forest and the southern loop of the Black Volta. The south-bound caravans, which supplied the trans-Saharan traffic with gold repaired to this growing commercial centre of Begho for their wares. By the beginning of the 15th century, a Mande colony was firmly established here.[11]

Another aspect of the pre-European international trade in Ghana was the Benin-Mina trade. By the 15th century, Elmina had grown into an important market, possibly stimulated by a resident vigorous Mandingo community.[12] The trade between Mina and Benin involved the exchange of gold from the former with slaves from the latter. This trade was taken over by the Portuguese from the 15th century.[13] The Portuguese also used a western trade route to the Cote d'Ivoire, from where they brought 'quaqua' cloth to Ghana.

With the coming of Europeans the gold trade in Ghana increased the country's economic activities. From the late 14th century, Europe was faced with the prospect of an acute gold shortage, and this, among other factors, caused Portugal to embark on West Coast exploration for Christian Europe to reach the source of the gold direct, instead of through Islamic Marghribian ports.[14] Naturally, the Portuguese were attracted to Elmina, already a centre for international (including the gold) trade. All their activities on the coast betrayed their twin aims of a quest for gold and a defence of Christianity. Thus, in 1481, they built Elmina Castle simultaneously as a base for potential religious campaigns, and a fortified trade post. Its strong bastion, like that of the second Portuguese Fort Sao Antonio at Axim, was pointing towards land to meet a possible infidel attack from the Mina Mandingo community, and the almost certain trade rivalry with the commercially-sophisticated local populace. Subsequently, Portuguese activities were even more geared to the quest for gold. Other forts built in the 16th century at the mouths of the Ankobra and the Prah rivers, which run through gold-bearing areas, were specifically meant for the gold trade, and was appropriately designed to ward off the frequent attacks by the local people. In the 1620s, the Portuguese tried unsuccessfully to gain direct access to the gold mines in the interior, first at Abrobi Hill near Komenda and then at the confluence of the Ankobra and Duma rivers.[15]

Activities of other European nations were also geared to the acquisition of gold. It was largely because of gold that the Dutch, Danes, Swedes, English, Brandenburgers and French entered the West African trade.[16] It was in 1637 that the Dutch launched their final asault on Elmina, then the gold mart of the West Coast. With the Portuguese thus driven away, the way was open for all the other powers to cash in and enter the competition for gold. Most of these European traders eventually repaired to Accra and Agona ports where they received Akyem gold through Akwamu middlemen.[17] Long before this, at the time of the English preparation to enter the competition in the 1550s, their monarch, King Edward IV, vividly referred to the West Coast trade as "exchange of baser merchandise for nobler".[18] Admittedly, the trade extended to other items including, ivory, wax, pepper and dye-wood, but gold was clearly the most important commodity.[19] By the end of the 15th century between 950 and 1350 kilogrammes of gold were carried annually by the Portuguese from Ghana. In the latter part of the 17th century altogether 1350 kilogrammes of gold were exported from Ghana by the various European powers.[20]

The Expanding Trade

Ghana's international trade with Europeans across the Atlantic expanded considerably since the 16th century. Demand for porters from Benin increased particularly as the volume of trade grew, and heavy items such as copper and iron were being imported from the coast. Trading caravans with their attendants grew in size. By the mid-18th century, a trading caravan from Akyem to the coast could number 2,000 men.[21]

Another aspect of the expanding trade was the multiplication of European trade-posts on a 480 kilometre long rocky coastline. Between the 16th century and 18th century about 60 castles, forts and lodges were built by the various European trading companies, first to protect their trade against Africans and later, as competition for the African trade increased, against each other.[22]

In addition to the early centres of trade with the north, i.e. Begho, Bono Mansu (1295),[23] Salaga, new depots developed along the Atlantic coast and in the heartland of the interior gold-bearing regions. Coastal areas which apart from Elmina witnessed considerable early trade were the western ports, particularly at the mouths of the Prah and Ankobra rivers. Several other trading ports also sprang up at Dixcove, Butri, Takoradi, etc.[24] Then came other trading centres such as Cape Coast, Winneba, Accra and Old Ningo. All these were important coastal markets which developed to serve the growing Atlantic trade. After the abandonment of Begho, sometime in the 17th century, Kumasi on a major trade route that extended south to the coast of Ghana and so by sea routes to the ports of Western Europe; and north to the ports of North Africa, grew rapidly, constituting an important factor in the rise of Asante.[25] Salaga and Kintampo at the crossroads of the trading streams of Hausa, Moshi and Wangara from the north also developed into rich commercial centres. The first traders to arrive here were the Wangara, who came for gold and kola nuts, and then the Hausa, who came for kola nuts. Hausa caravans approaching Salaga or Kintampo would often number 3000 persons, carrying indigo, cloths woven in the Hausa fashion, cattle and sheep.[26] The kola nuts they carried from these depots on their way back to the north was next to gold as an item of the growing international trade. No wonder these towns became emporia of great wealth and repute.

The contribution of kola nuts to the expanding international trade in Ghana was considerable. Kola nuts constituted the first agriculture export and, as already said, were sent north where their use in the desert conditions of the Sahara served as a strong link between Ghana and the outside world. Indeed, the origins of the Wangara stream of the traffic is put as early as 11th century and that of Hausa no later than the 13th century.[27] The nuts were transported on asses to Timbuktu and Kano, where they were exchanged for European goods such as scissors, paper, needles, calico etc. It was from these Western Sudanese centres that the kola nuts were further distributed throughout the Sahara desert and the major North African ports.[28]

This growing trade greatly benefited from the development of currencies. As early as the 15th century, possibly earlier, parts of Ghana started using cowry shells as currencies. These shells originated from the Indian Ocean and their use as currency was already in the Western Sudan by the 14th century. It was from here that they spread south to Hausaland and northern Ghana. On the coast, the Portuguese used cowry shells for their coastwise trade during the 16th century. Cowries thus became the chief medium of exchange in the coastal trading centres, and by the 17th century their use must have already penetrated the hinterland. The Akwamu empire was by then exchanging slaves for cowries. Gold dust was also used as currency but it was not as widespread as cowries. The only other currency known at this time in Ghana was a type of iron currency used in Asante up to the end of the 16th century.[29]

Results of the Expanding Trade
As already indicated, the very first result of the growing international trade was the drawing of Ghana into the world economy. From that time onwards, the course of economic activity in Ghana has been constantly influenced by the outside world. During the gold era, favourable conditions existed for Ghanaians to channel these influences into productive sectors of the economy. So, the good effects of these foreign contacts outweighed the bad.

In the first place, there was considerable increase in economic activity in the country. This could be seen in the need to import labour. Naturally, rapid population growth had accompanied the fast economic development from the late stone technology through the iron age. Consequently, the need to import more labour, during the gold era, was indicative of an even faster growing economy in the country. As already seen, the labour was imported from Benin along with other items. The people involved were captives from the numerous Benin wars in the 16th and 17th centuries. This background of the imported labour force needs to be stressed as in all probability domestic slavery and pawning system in Ghana evolved from this quest for labour. In other words, the much criticized domestic slavery and pawning were originally no more than a system of labour force needed in a rapidly-growing economy, the stigma of slavery coming in only because of an accidental captive origin of the imported labour force.

This turn of events in Ghana led to the formulation of a viable labour policy by which the country built up population as a source of labour and social strength,[30] and this contributed in no small measure to the expansion of the economy. Thus, if population increase was a major result of the expanding trade, the specialization of this population in various crafts and industries was an even more important result. Various localities specialized in one industry or the other. So, fishing and salt-manufacturing developed along the coast; farming in the wet forested hinterland, cattle-rearing in the savannah areas, weaving, pottery where suitable raw materials existed. Places like Wassa and Akyem concentrated on gold mining.[31] A portion of the imported labour force was drafted into the porterage of goods to and from the coast. They formed part of the very large trading caravans then typical of Ghana's trading systems.

The Rise of Crafts, Extractive and Manufacturing Industries
By the term crafts, extractive and manufacturing industries we are here referring to the art of extracting metals and minerals from the earth, wood and other forest products from forests, and of making things mainly by hand out of the raw materials available to Ghanaians from agriculture, forestry and mining. What follows is in fact a description of the origins of a cottage, extractive and manufacturing industries, arts and crafts, as we designate them in the 19th and 20th centuries.

Even though the origins of iron workings precede the period of expanding trade, their development continued throughout, and were largely stimulated by, the gold era. Furthermore, in order to see the early development of crafts, extractive and manufacturing industries as a whole, we shall have to consider here, along with others, the development of iron craft from its origins.

Iron Extraction and Mongery
Concrete evidence of the art of extracting iron from its ore exists in the remains of iron smelting kilns with deposits of iron slag at hilltop sites all over the country. In association with these exhibits, one usually finds pottery fragments clearly depicting settlements devoted to iron smelting. Achimota at the edge of the Accra plains, Akpafu in the Volta Region and the hills around Cape

Coast in the Central Region were just a few of the better known iron smelting sites in Ghana.[32]

Iron mongery was bound to be so widespread because apart from metal specialists there were others such as hunters who had to acquire the knowledge of iron workings. Hunting involved learning to repair guns. In some parts of the Volta Region, the young apprentice hunter had to learn how to smelt iron and prepare his own cartridges and cutlasses.[33] As Europeans began to import iron and copper bars into Ghana, there was tremendous increase in the forging of various types of metal tools for household, agricultural and mining purposes. Hoes, spears, picks and axes etc. were made in the various blacksmithing shops.

Gold Mining and Smithery
The gold mining industry was restricted largely to the Akan-speaking areas, but probably involved a lot more people than did iron. Like iron, however, gold extraction was shrouded in secrecy, and strict rules governed its operation. Gold was associated with magic. And yet the extraction of gold from its rock was continually being demonstrated by Nature itself in the alluvial deposits on river beds within the auriferous regions. So, mining for gold started with the washing method. Baskets were used to sift alluvial deposits from river beds and the particles of gold were left behind. The next step was for the people to extract the gold from its rock themselves. In this case, they first had to mine the rock from underground. This Akan gold production, as we have seen, began before the 16th century and involved the development of the open pit system of mining which was highly labour intensive.[34] The rocks were first broken into pieces and then smelted down to separate gold from its matrix.

Goldsmithery was equally ancient, and the gold extracted from the rock was used to make different types of figurines and objects, including chiefs' paraphernalia, bracelets, finger-rings, brooches, and zodiac rings for the elite in society. The goldsmith's skill was highly respected by the community. It was jealously guarded and passed down the generations only through very formal and difficult apprenticeship. Like other group crafts, goldsmithery thrived within craft guilds associations buttressed by social and political cohesion. The powerful ruler of such a state acted as patron and the artists were inspired to produce some of the finest works imaginable. This was why in Ghana we find a highly-developed artistic craftmanship in the powerful kingdom of Asante.[35]

Pottery

Pottery was one of the industries vital to a growing economy. And although its development in a locality depended on the availability of suitable clay, there were other factors which strongly promoted the setting up of pottery industries. In traditional education, for instance, great emphasis was placed on training people as potters. The community had great need of pots for storage purposes, both domestic and commercial, for cooking and serving meals. Three important uses in the area of commercial storage were as containers for dye made from barks of trees, for locally-made salt and finally for palm oil. Domestic storage involved using pots as water holders.[36]

A further importance of pottery was its backward linkage effects. Even though pottery was the preserve of women, a number of industries by men was essential for the smooth operation of the pottery business. Some of these backward linkages were the manufacture of tools for shaping and smoothening pots. A special framework and net used for carrying pots to market also necessitated a thriving industry in pot making areas.[37]

Pottery was a widespread industry in Ghana, found not just on iron smelting sites, as already indicated, but practically on all settlements of some importance. However, it was only certain areas that specialized in it. In Southern Ghana, Shailand was a notable pot-making area. Here pot-making was one of the domestic duties of women and they made over 35 different kinds of pots.[38]

Cloth Making

Cloth making started with the use of barks of certain trees which when skilfully treated yielded a type of course cloth worn round the loins. Animal skins were also worn as cloth. But these habits did not persist. The cotton tree is indigenous and thrived both in the savannah and the forest areas, and it did not take long for West Africans to discover the usefulness of the cotton fibre. The cultivation of the tree both in the forest and in the savannah constituted an early agricultural practice and this was soon followed by the acquisition of the technique of spinning, most probably through invention. Areas where the cotton tree established itself quite early in the history of Ghanaian agriculture include the Volta Region in the Alavanyo district, Northern Ghana and the area north of Kumasi in Asante. Cultivation of the cotton tree in these areas became a regular economic activity. So did the spinning of yarns and the weaving of a cotton cloth far superior to its predecessor. Of the three regions, Northern Ghana and the Volta Region continued the industry on individaul basis and not much change was noticeable here throughout the gold era. But in Asante at Bonwire spectacular changes occurred in the industry and transformed it into a national occupation.[39]

The people of Bonwire were said to have hailed from Denkyera and on leaving there moved around until they finally settled down a little to the north of Kumasi. They developed the art of weaving the kente with cotton yarns. They grew their own cotton and spun their own yarns. As they were forest dwellers, they soon learnt how to make dyes from the barks of certain forest trees. They dyed the yarns in various colours and thus invented the colourful kente that we know today. It was not long before they discovered silky yarns to make the kente the beautiful cloth that it is today.[40]

The perfection of the art of weaving kente in Bonwire came with royal patronage in Osei Tutu's time. The Asantehene's patronage meant that the chief weavers at Bonwire had to direct the business solely for the execution of royal orders. If any chief wanted kente, he could have it woven by these patented Bonwire weavers with the Asantehene's permission. No weaving could be done for the common people as before. Great care was taken to produce work of the first quality in order to satisfy the royal taste. This was how Bonwire acquired its fame as a notable weaving centre in Ghana. Further changes were to come but these will have to be considered in a later chapter.

Salt Making
Far into the distant past, coastal lagoons and the sea served as the source of salt for the inhabitants of the sea board and the hinterland as well. Particularly in the Keta lagoon ideal conditions existed for the natural formation of salt grains on the beds of the

lagoon through evaporation of the lagoon in the hot tropical sun. The salt left behind on the dry beds was collected and heaped on the banks of the lagoon, ready for sale.

From this natural phenomenon which occurred in several other places like Ada and Elmina, some coastal communities learnt to make salt themselves using stagnant brackish water behind the coast line. This involved boiling the brine in large earthen pots till all the water evaporated leaving the grains of salt behind.

Quite often, such communities were also fishermen in the lagoons, rivers and the sea. They used some of the salt to cure the fish and transported both commodities up the rivers or by forest paths into the hinterland where they exchanged them for foodstuff.

Woodworks
Another useful occupation was woodworks. The availability of different species of useful woods in Ghanaian forests was realized by the people quite early in their history. When iron tools became available wood carving grew into a viable occupation. Thus, even though during these early days the uses of wood were limited to carved objects, there was a wide range of them. The earliest were religious objects like fertility dolls and doll size replacements for dead twins. There were also stools, snuff boxes, walking sticks, handles for hoes and cutlasses, doors and indoor games equipment. Carving of several other useful appliances went on. Canoes for fishing and river transport were dug out of large tree trunks. Wooden trays and other receptacles as well as mortars and pestles were also carved from different types of trees in the forest. This involved a great deal of acquaintance with the different species in the forest.

To a large extent, then, social and economic life depended on the use of wood. Even in these early days, social life seemed impossible without wooden objects and utensils; and the fact that craftsmen came up so early with all these products is a reflection of the level of economic prosperity. Most of these wooden products thus first came into existence at the heyday of the gold era, when prosperity made financing more sophisticated tools and appliances possible and helped the people make improvement in their social life.

Minor Industries

Several minor industries also sprang up before the 17th century and helped to improve the quality of life. Most of them were either forward or backward linkages of the industries already discussed above. Potters, weavers and wood-carvers needed the services of several other workers to get the tools and materials for their operations. And to dispose of their products, they needed services of a different set of workers. Hence, the work of leather workers, rope makers and boat-builders etc. came in handy.[41]

All these professions and the growing trade itself needed technical services. The best example of a technical service provided for both the internal and the international trade was the Asante gold weights, which were items of local manufacture and used for measuring gold dust.[42] As Ghana's economy grew, signs of prosperity other than technical services began to appear in various forms. Just as the growing trade nurtured a class of labourers in the porterage and mining businesses, so it stimulated the emergence of a class of entrepreneurs. The manufacture of gold and silver and, in particular, iron goods were complicated, and required the services of an entrepreneurial class to supervise the production process from the mining of the ore to the finished goods. The earliest entrepreneurial classes in Ghana were the gold and silver smiths, established all over the gold mining regions.

Sometimes, the guild system which saw the attainment of high craftmanship in the various professions was extended to the marketing of the goods. They were often referred to as market associations, and they developed special skills in disposing off the finished goods. These thus developed into entrepreneurial groups.

The expansion of trade and commerce physically involved the introduction of long-distance trade following the full establishment of short distance trade between the neighbouring states, districts or villages. Long-distance trade crossed the borders of one or more states to distant markets. The northern traffic in gold and kola nuts, the southern traffic between the interior and the coast and the Benin-Mina trade were all long-distance trade.

The organization of such a trade involved a great deal of preparations. The caravans were large and took time to assemble. Their protection through hostile country was a costly affair. Furthermore, long-distance trade involved expensive items as iron, gold and silver goods, whose manufacture, as we have seen, was complicated, requiring supervision by an entrepreneurial class. Naturally, long-distance trade was made possible by the patronage of a small but wealthy class of citizens who alone could pay for the expensive goods and services provided. During the gold era this wealthy class was thus useful in the economic development of Ghana.

Rapid Development in Agriculture

The establishment of agriculture in Ghana starting around 500 BC, to some extent, undid the ill-effects of Ghana missing the bronze age. This resulted in the cultivation of the indigenous crops discussed above. Gradual development came through accumulation of farming and related experiences covering knowledge of wild fruits, crops and weather problems in cultivating them as well as outbreaks of pests and diseases. Accumulated experience in these areas came with improved agricultural practices, even though the latter was often camouflaged with fetish beliefs. Thus, the people adopted forest reserves but called them sacred forests for the gods and spirits. Again, it was experience that, quite early in their agricultural history, taught the people, for instance, how to remove prussic acid from cassava with urine to make it edible.[43]

The gold trade stimulated more agricultural development. The various foreign contacts that the people established in the course of the trade was a fertile source of new ideas which influenced agriculture, decisively. There was first and foremost improvement in farming methods and techniques which came with new tools. The trading caravans of Arabs and Moors which entered Ghana[44] from the north included non-traders like the escorts or mounted lancers, religious personnel and farmers. So the strangers' quarters that these traders established in such trading depots like Salaga and Kintampo became settlements with full communal facilities. New ideas of cultivation were conveyed by these settlers to the local population who gradually accepted and practised the new methods, particularly since the needed iron tools also came with the strangers. The Arabs and Moors also brought new crops with them.

From the 15th century when Europeans arrived at the coast, a similar influence was established on agriculture. The period when the gold trade flourished in places like the Bono Kingdom and in the Atlantic ports was also the period of fast agricultural growth, namely, the 16th and 17th centuries, but particularly between

1612 and 1640 when the gold trade soared. So, areas of thriving agriculture also corresponded to those of prosperous gold trading. The areas of concentrated European trading activities such as between Sekondi and Winneba witnessed early agricultural development as the Portuguese built gardens around their forts, the Danes experimented with their botanic gardens, and both thus influenced the local agricultural skills acquired since New Stone and early Iron Ages. Indeed, Ghana's ancient farming tradition originated from here with farming groups moving to the eastern part of the country during the Asante wars and establishing themselves in the then relatively more peaceful eastern districts.

Meanwhile, these districts had their own incentives for a strong agricultural tradition. When the Danes entered the West Coast gold trade they caused tracts of land to be cleared in the Accra area and they employed the inhabitants in a form of plantation farming. They encouraged them to extend their farming activities and grow more grain for export to Europe. This stimulated farming quite early in the neighbourhood of the Accra plains, particularly in the Akwapem and Krobo districts. With the arrival of the Western and Central Districts farming groups, therefore, a strong foundation was laid in these areas for sound agricultural practices.[4,5]

An important aspect of this growing agriculture was the introduction of new crops into Ghana by Arabs from the north and Europeans from the south. The earlier crops developed included bananas, plantains, yams, oil palm, rice and cotton. The crops introduced by the Europeans included maize, millet, sweet potatoes, cassava, groundnuts, tomatoes, oranges and apples which the Portuguese brought in from South America and elsewhere.

NOTES

1. The Gold Coast Chamber of Mines 1950. *Gold from the Gold Coast*, p. 29.
2. De Kun, Nicolas 1965. *The Mineral Resources of Africa*, p. 90. New York: Elsevier Publishing Company; *West Africa*, October 1949.
3. De Kun, Nicolas 1965. *Op. cit.*, p. 61. Lode is primary deposit in which the gold occurs. The other two sources of gold in Ghana, i.e. oxidized ore out-crops and alluvial deposits are results of weather action on lode.

4. Birmingham, Walter, Neustadt, L. and Omaboe, E. N. (ed.) 1966. *A Study of Contemporary Ghana, Vol. I: The Economy of Ghana*, p. 250. London: Allen and Unwin Ltd.
5. The Gold Coast Chamber of Mines 1950. *Op. cit.*, pp. 8–9; De Kun, Nicolas 1965. *Op. cit.*, pp. 309–314.
6. Rodney, Walter 1969. Gold and slaves on the Gold Coast. *Transactions of the Historical Society of Ghana* X 13–28.
7. *Ibid.*
8. Van Dantzig, Albert 1980. *Forts and Castles of Ghana*, p. 3. Accra: Sedco Publishing Co. Ltd.
9. Junner, N. R. 1973. *Gold in the Gold Coast*. pp. 1–5, Accra: Ghana Geological Survey Department.
10. Rodney, Walter 1969. *Op. cit.*
11. Wilks, Ivor 1961. The northern factor in Ashanti history; Begho and the Mande. *Journal of African History* II(I): 25–34.
12. Van Dantzig, Albert 1980. *Op. cit.*, p. 3.
13. Rodney, Walter 1969. *Op. cit.*
14. Wilks, Ivor 1961. *Op. cit.*
15. Van Dantzig, Albert 1980. *Op cit.*, pp. 6–8.
16. Rodney, Walter 1969. *Op. cit.*
17. *Ibid.*
18. Kleist, Alice, M. 1957. The English African trade under the Tudors. *Transactions of the Historical Society of Ghana* 111 (2): 137–150.
19. Van Dantzig, Albert 1980. *Op. cit.*, p. 12
20. Rodney, Walter 1969. *Op. cit.*
21. *Ibid.*
22. Van Dantzig, Albert 1980. *Op. cit.*, p. vii.
23. La Anyane, S. 1963. *Op. cit.*, p. 7.
24. Van Dantzig, Albert 1973. The Ankobra Gold interest. *Transactions of the Historical Society of Ghana* xiv (2): 169–185.
25. Wilks, Ivor 1961. *Op. cit.*
26 Rouch, Jean 1955. *Notes on Migrations into the Gold Coast, 1st Report of the Mission Carried out in the Gold Coast from March to December 1954, from CNRS* Paris: Mise de L'Homme.
27. Boahen, Adu 1961. Ghana kola trade. *Ghana Notes and Queries* 1: 8–10.
28. *Ibid.*
29. Daaku, K.Y. 1961. Pre-European currencies of West Africa and Western Sudan. *Ghana Notes and Queries* 2: 12–14.
30. Rodney, Walter 1969. *Op. cit.*
31. *Ibid.*
32. Penfold, D. A. 1971. Excavation of an iron-smelting site at Cape Coast. *Transactions of the Historical Society of Ghana* xii: 1–5.
33. Kwamena-Poh, M. A. 1975. The traditional informal system of education in pre-colonial Ghana. *Presence Africaine* 95 (3): 269–283.
34. Rodney, Walter 1969. *Op. cit.*

35. Kwamena-Poh, M. A. 1975. *Op. cit.*
36. *Ibid.*
37. *Ibid.*
38. *Ibid.*
39. *See* Danquah, Moses 1958. The saga of the Kente and how it is worn. *The Ghanaian* (3): 24, 25, 38.
40. *Ibid.*
41. *See* Kwamena-Poh, M. A. 1975. *Op. cit.*
42. Agbodeka, Francis 1986. *Op. cit.*
43. La Anyane, S. 1963. *Op. cit.*, p. 5.
44. *Ibid.*, p. 9.
45. *Ibid.*, pp. 9–10.

Chapter 3

THE SLAVE TRADE ERA

Origins of the Atlantic Slave Trade
Before the arrival of Europeans in the 15th century, the growing African economy had stimulated the growth of class distinctions which, as we have seen included porters and labourers as well as pawns. These people on the lowest rank of the social ladder often got there through captivity and easily fell victims of social oppression. Until European influence affected the social structure, however, these 'serfs' virtually formed part of the families they served and sometimes through hard work and good character attained responsible positions in them.

As their exploration from Upper Guinea to Lower Guinea progressed with the 15th century, the Portuguese cultivated the habit of taking back a few Africans on each trip to serve in rich households in Europe. So began the activity of kidnapping Africans which started off the Atlantic slave trade. Later, most of the slaves exported were war captives, and it was to a large extent the lowly in the society who suffered this terrible fate. Occasionally, a member of the ruling class might fall a victim. The number of victims generally increased as their export to the New World as slaves began. In South America, they worked in gold and silver mines but later on sugar plantations. If the European traders made huge profits in the triangular trade, it was the elite in Africa itself that benefited at the expense of pawns or ordinary folk. The role of the rich as entrepreneurs in society was now perverted into one of depleting the very labour force that helped to create their wealth. The sound labour policy of the gold era was abandoned with serious repercussions on the entire economy.

Even though it was the Portuguese who started the slave trade it soon became their national policy to restrain their companies and traders in Ghana from participating in it. They could of course carry on the trade elsewhere in West Africa. The reason for this was to reserve Ghana for the gold trade on which, so far, the economy of Europe was based.

The other European nations had to follow the Portuguese example. The Dutch, in particular, kept the slave trade out of Ghana to concentrate on the gold trade. This emphasis on the gold trade meant that, for most of the 17th century, whenever they had no gold from Ghana, then all the Dutch were left with were cloth and beads from other parts of West Africa.[1]

Expansion of the Slave Trade

But all along, there were important reasons why the slave trade should increase. The Volta Region of Ghana had no gold, which existed, as already indicated, only west of the Volta. The slave trade initiated by the Portuguese in the 15th century persisted in spite of European national efforts to exclude it from Ghana, and the Volta Region, in particular, embraced it. It did not mean that this Region of Ghana valued its labour force less; it was merely a question of survival and slaves provided the means for that purpose. Social and political differences between coastal and interior elements of the Volta Region population fanned the waylaying of unwary travellers and traders. It was these hostilities that kept streams of captives arriving at the small seaports in the Keta district for sale to Europeans. Other captives were simply the victims of inter-village conflicts, especially among the coastal states.

Furthermore, regions west of the Volta where gold trade thrived during the 17th century began gradually to turn to the slave trade. One such area was the Accra region, so well endowed with a rich gold-producing hinterland. After 1678, with the military defeat of Accra by Akwamu, the former became isolated from the gold-producing areas. Ports west of Accra like Senya Bereku also saw their gold trade decline. Thus, the slave trade tended to increase in all these areas.

Akwamu which since the second half of the 17th century had grown into a powerful kingdom entered the gold trade and directed it to Accra. Gradually, Akwamu's attention was being turned to the Volta as its outlet to the European trading posts east of Accra. The reason for shifting eastwards to the Volta was that Akwamu had never established control over the gold-producing areas to its west because of the great influence of Akyem and was no more than a middleman in the gold trade going southwards. In face of the great political power of Akyem, Akwamu's middleman position was tenuous and this was why Akwamu was looking east for the control of trade there. It became engrossed in the politics and warfare of the Lower Volta basin. Akwamu allied with Anlo and consequently co-operated with Anlo's proteges, Kwahu and Agotime, against Ada, Popo and Krepe. It was the Krepe and the Mahis to their north that were often sold on the Lower Volta as slaves.[2] Akwamu's participation in the affairs of the Volta states thus constituted the activities of an expansionist power boosting the slave trade. Akwamu in fact came to specialize in the slave trade and when it fell in 1734 it left the imperial legacy of the slave trade in the economic field, just as it left that of statecraft in the political. These events caused the Akan states west of the Volta to increasingly abandon the gold for the slave trade.

Another source of the growing slave trade was Asante. Asante law and custom forbad enslaving Asante citizens. So the slaves that were brought down to Cape Coast Castle came from the territories to the north of this powerful kingdom, which organized their purchase from the collecting market of Salaga, or acquired them as tributes or captives of war. Prior to this method of disposal of captives, the Asante kingdom kept them for various purposes, but found their upkeep expensive. The coming of the European slave trade presented to the Asantehene an easy option, though not the best, in handling this class of people. Accordingly, the slaves were now marched to the reselling market of Manso where Fante and Ga merchants acquired them and took them to the European slave traders on the coast.

Also important for the growth of the slave trade in the Akan area was the development of events in Fanteland. Here, in the early years of the 18th century the Borbor Fante attacked and conquered the non-Borbor Fante states such as Eguafo, Fetu, Asebu and Agona with the aim of seizing middleman control of the trading paths between the coast and the interior. This resulted in the waging of numerous wars which stifled gold production and which occasioned the influx of firearms and the acquisition of numerous war captives whom the Fante sold to the Europeans in exchange for more firearms. Thus, the stream of slaves reaching the coast for sale from the far interior was now increased by the Fante wars, which drastically reduced the gold to the benefit of the slave trade.

It was changes in European attitude to the slave trade that finally opened the flood gates of the trade in Ghana. As early as the 6th decade of the 17th century, the English had begun a move to increase European demand for slaves in Ghana This move was born of a continuing ill-fortune in the English gold trade and the

need for their traders to turn to the slave trade for compensation. Furthermore, the English needed slaves at this time to work their West Indian plantations. At first, however, it was just gun-running that the English sponsored on the coast and this was often done, not by the members of the official trading company, but by English interlopers. Large supplies of firearms, of course, promoted the slave trade and soon official English trading personnel vied with the interlopers in fostering the inhuman trade in slaves. By the beginning of the 18th century, the English Royal African Company decided to make Ghana the main source for the Atlantic Slave Trade and Cape Coast the centre of their slave purchases in the country.[3] The Ghanaian-English trade became competitive and other European traders had to find an answer to this competition. About the second decade of the 18th century, the Dutch reacted by relaxing their merchantile rules that had hitherto restricted their share of the slave trade in Ghana. So their West India Company ships began to load slaves in Elmina on their eastward voyages.[4]

Slaves reached the European buyers at various points along the coast of Ghana. The centres for the purchase of slaves from the Volta Region and Akwamu were in the same area. The coastal markets used by Anlo and Akwamu were situated between Aflao and Ningo, where some half a dozen towns, i.e. Aflao, Keta, Woe, Anloga, Ada and Ningo, swarmed with slave dealers. Sometimes, even Popo captives were exported through this region and the total number of slave exports through this Keta-Ada district was appreciable.

Some slaves from Asante and later all slaves from Fante reached the coast at the central district ports, particularly Cape Coast Castle and Anomabu, but as the 18th century progressed, Asante slave trade shifted to the coast from Christiansborg to Aflao. There was no doubt that by the early part of the 18th century, the slave trade was already booming in Ghana. Reports in 1706 indicate that Cape Coast Castle alone exported 10,198 captives in 2½ years, while the annual figure for Anomabu was 5,000 slaves. It is estimated that all the various outlets on the African continent exported to the New World about 11 million slaves. Many more were lost through slave raids, and death during the march to the coast and the Middle Passage. Altogether, Africa must have lost close to 20 million peoples during the three centuries of the Atlantic Slave Trade.

The spectacular expansion of the slave trade was preceded by the trade in gold and accompanied by other forms of trade based on forest exploitation or agriculture. One of the forest products involved was timber.

Natural conditions existed for trade in timber. The forests in Ghana were then as now endowed with many species of wood, some of them with outstanding high market value; because of their usefulness in the construction business and for the expensive architectural taste of a growing industrial and affluent society in Europe. These forests, whether close to the seaboard or some distance from it, were linked to the European trading posts by ancient rivers and streams, which flooded their basins during heavy tropical downpours and provided easy transportation for logs floating downstream to the seaboard. European merchants were thus able to organize an early log export business from Ghana, particularly in the western districts where such rivers as Prah, Ankobra and Tano provided this important facility for early European trade. These rivers did not just provide water transport for logs, but also aided European penetration, however shallow, of an otherwise totally impenetrable tropical forest.

The timber trade was different from the gold trade in that the felling of trees was, unlike the digging of gold, initiated by the more technically-advanced Europeans, and this altogether excluded Africans from the trade. It was thus purely exploitative, all profits going to the visitors only. The volume of this early timber trade is difficult to assess but there are indications that the 18th century beginning was a worthy forerunner of the spectacular 19th century European exploitation of tropical forests.

Included in the forest products was ivory which even though of more exclusive use was just as valued as, if not more than, timber. Ivory was used to decorate the homes of the landed gentry in 18th century Europe and later in the 19th century those of the *nouveaux riche* as well. So the trade was comparatively small in volume as it was meant to satisfy the taste of only the rich few. Even if the number had been bigger, collecting ivory was more tedious than catching slaves, and the supply of elephant tusks to the trading posts was bound to be disrupted by the slave raiders. Besides, the slave trade was backed by chiefs and elders while ivory collection was organized by farmers who sometimes hunted down the elephants only when they destroyed their farms. So the African ivory collectors were much less organized and business-like than the patrons of the slave trade.

However, Ghanaian ivory traders soon realized the keeness of the Europeans for elephant teeth. So like other expensive tropical goods, long distance trade came to be organized for ivory. The traders acquired the tusks from well-known elephant hunters. They then formed trading caravans. These trading caravans emerged from different parts of the Ghana forest carrying ivory and other forest products to the European trading posts. Two areas noted for large populations of elephants were the western districts along the Cote d'Ivoire border and the Afram Plains. Centres of ivory sale to Europeans were thus the western districts ports and trading posts immediately west of Accra, and the east as far as Aflao.

If ivory collection was casual, the trade itself did have one advantage, that of African participation and consequent local share, however small, in the profits realized. More important was African control of the trade at its source, and he could, if he so wished, ignore European tastes and spare "his" elephants. He could not exercise this kind of control in the case of timber, and so could not prevent the ruthless exploitation of this important natural resource in Ghana.

Three different crops which received some attention during the slave trade era were Indian corn, palm nut and cassava. An indigenous cereal that appeared on the West African scene as early as the domestication period was Guinea corn. But during the slave trade era it was a different species of corn introduced into Ghana from the East that was exported. Indian corn must have reached West Africa latest by the 13th century, AD, brought in by Arab traders across the Sahara. By the 17th and 18th centuries, its cultivation in Ghana was not only well-established but also preferred to the local variety. Indian corn proved more high yielding. Some of it was grown in European experimental gardens. Its export was to provide food for the slaves on the coast, the Middle Passage and even in the New World.

As food for slaves, however, cassava was preferred to corn. Cassava was a hardier plant; it could withstand all soil and weather conditions. This was precisely why the Portuguese introduced it into West Africa from Brazil. By the 16th century, cassava must have been well established in Ghana. Its spread into all parts of the country was spectacular and it came to be a staple crop for most Ghanaians.

Another food item important for the slave trade was palm oil. It was an important item in the diet of the local people and the European slave dealers took care to include it in the meals for their slaves. With this crop, all that needed to be done was to improve the yield, since it was indigenous and already adapted to the soil and climatic conditions of Ghana. But in spite of this advantage, palm oil output at this time was not much better than Indian corn or cassava. The problem was that agriculture as a whole suffered during the slave trade era, as discussed below. So the crops grown during this era could not develop fast even where their cultivation was important for the slave trade itself. At best, enough was produced for the local population. Quite often, there was not enough to go round, let alone a surplus to generate further economic activity.

In exchange for these goods, Ghana imported a variety of goods ranging from textiles to paints; some of the most important commodities were textiles, canvas, linseed tar, lead, brass, paints and barrels.[5] Others were firearms, gunpowder, tobacco and rum. These goods came from Europe. From the northern traffic came indigo and Hausa cloth, some cattle and sheep.[6] These were brought by Hausa caravans from Kano.

Trade Routes

There were four major routes from the interior to the sea coast. Three of these emerged from the rich Asante capital, Kumasi, passing through several hamlets and towns in the intermediary states of the country to the sea coast at (a) Assini, Axim or Dixcove and other smaller ports in the western districts; (b) Elmina, Cape Coast and Anomabu in the central districts; (c) Accra and the leeward stations as far as Aflao on the borders of the Popo country. The fourth route which by-passed Kumasi used the Volta basin mainly till it fanned out in the Lower Volta area, a branch going west to Christiansborg, Ningo and Ada, and another branch going direct to the Anlo sea ports.

Trade routes which served the earlier gold and ivory trade came to be used for the slave trade too. So in fact, slaves were exported through all the ports mentioned above. But generally, more gold tended to reach the coast through the western trade routes, and more slaves through the eastern ones. Ivory was equally distributed to all parts.

The two major eastern trade routes carried mainly ivory and slaves. One came from Kumasi through Akyem, Akwapem to Accra and environs. Asante used this to bring in ivory, gold and slaves to Christiansborg. The other from as far north as Salaga and the Brong Confederation only passed through Akwapem to Accra, Ningo and the leeward European establishments, such as Prampram and Ada.[7]

Ada is situated at the mouth of the Volta, in the lower reaches of which a complicated trade network developed during the 17th and 18th centuries. Several factors made Ada one of the best places in Ghana for the slave trade. Its position at the mouth of the Lower Volta, which washed the shores of great slaving states of the Volta Region was very convenient for two reasons. First, its easy defence by European men-of-war from both the sea and the river made it into a good slave strong-hold. Secondly, cheap and easy river transportation of slaves in canoes down the river to the stronghold was no doubt appreciated by the Danes who built Fort Kongensten there to make it a leading slave trading post in Ghana.

Importantly, Ada had its share of the direct Asante trade exports of ivory, gold and slaves, as already discussed above. Yet, there was another Asante-controlled trade reaching Ada through Akwamu which supervised this trade in the interest of the Asantehene during the late 18th century. This particular link was partly forged by the Adas themselves as great traders, carrying large quantities of salt and dried fish to the Akwamus living on the Volta islands and further up the river to other riverine communities. Finally, slaves reached Ada from Agotime, Adaklu, Nyive and Takla.

Kwahu, a large and impressive kingdom on the Volta beyond Akwamu is said to have sent trade goods down the river to the coast, mostly to the Anlo country east of the river, but a good portion of it found its way to the commanding Fort Kongensten at Ada.[8]

Even though the slaving states of the Volta Region sent some of their human cargoes down the Volta to Ada, much of the trade from the Krepe-Agotime area went to the Anlo country as already indicated earlier in this chapter. The sources of this trade included the traditional states of Krepe, Sokode, Ave, Agu, Tove, Gble, Seve, and Agotime. The sizes of these republics varied from 12 to 24 small subject towns. The 18th century saw these communities busily exporting slaves which were marched to the Anlo republic on the sea coast. The points at which the slaves emerged as already discussed were Anloga, Woe, Keta and Aflao. Some of this trade of course went to Little Popo. Each of these coastal towns had Danish lodges for handling the slave trade. Keta was the largest post, and with its Danish Fort Prinsensten, drew most of the slave trade from the Ewe interior.[9]

Decline of Arts and Crafts, Extractive, Manufacturing and Agricultural Industries

Iron smelting which could have developed as a basic industry in Ghana collapsed totally by the end of the 18th century. It is true that decline in the iron-smelting industry started before the heyday of the slave trade, but the latter hastened the end of this very basis of industrial growth.

Iron smelting, as a specialization, started very early, but the conditions for its growth were eroded by importation into Ghana of iron bars by European slave traders. Iron-smelting methods in Ghana, as in other parts of West Africa, were primitive and uneconomical. It has been shown that 102 kilograms of charcoal and 90 kilograms of iron ore were needed to produce 75 kilograms of forged iron.[10] Thus, like the Igbo smiths of Eastern Nigeria, Ghanaian iron smiths abandoned their professions and consequently, the traditional hilltop iron-smelting settlements that were set on the path of progress, however hard, for the more easy-going and dependent communities around European forts and castles at such places as Elmina, Cape Coast and Accra. This move of traditional settlements to European trading posts on the sea coast was the one act that destroyed the basis of Ghana's future industrial and technological advancement. The art of tool-making which was basic to the growth of industry declined with the increasing dependence of the people on imported European tools.

Since tool-making skills were impaired, the growth of industries like manufacturing industries, and even agricultural industries which depended on the use of improved tools were also stunted. It meant that the early 17th century specialization in Ghanaian society, already referred to, was now thwarted and the various cottage manufacturing industries remained at the rudimentary stage, making possible their replacement by European imports. Such manufacturing and extractive industries as pottery, boat-making and salt-making and agricultural industries like farming, fishing and animal husbandry were starved of progress because of the lack of effective tools and technology.

Mining which was then, and still is, another important branch of industry in Ghana also suffered as the local tool and technological development could not match the increasing problems posed by under-surface mining. Here, too, imported European technology replaced rather than supplemented ancient African efforts. In the case of mining, particularly gold mining, a solid local beginning had been laid. A good portion of the early labour imports from Benin were drafted into the African gold mines, so as to build up a strong reserve of skill in gold mining. Indeed, the Ghanaian traditional authorities took great care to give the mining population the stability needed for the mining business to the extent of importing females from Benin for the mining settlements. This was a sound labour policy evolved by the well-structured Akan societies whose chiefs and elite controlled the economy and maintained communal solidarity.[11] But the Atlantic Slave Trade corrupted this traditional leadership and removed the labour force both skilled and unskilled from the gold-producing sector, weakening the extractive industry to fall as a prize to 19th century European adventurers. Briefly therefore, an early African start towards progress in these key areas was thwarted by the Atlantic Slave Trade.

Loss of population generally was as disastrous for Ghana as the loss of skilled labour in the manufacturing industries. The entire population was a farming community. Even where they were engaged on some manufacturing industries, they still farmed in their spare time. To take away the young and the vigorous for sale as slaves, therefore, meant considerable loss to the premier economic activity — farming. In this respect, the loss in population was not merely those captured and sold to the European slave traders, but also those who died during the slave raids or during the difficult march to the coast. Furthermore, agriculture being a peace time occupation suffered because of the uncertainty created by raids. The frequent destruction of crops and the sudden seizure of farmers by slave raiders created despondency and kept agriculture at the rudimentary stage for a long time. Besides, the incessant inter ethnic warfare and rivalry during the slave raiding period unsettled farming[12] and, for that matter, crafts and industry as well.

General Results of the Slave Trade

Generally, the slave trade brought untold disaster to Ghana. The time that it replaced the gold trade in Ghana was the period Europeans valued it above the gold trade as the main support of their economy. In Ghana on the contrary it was the bane of the economy. The people realized it and in spite of being forced into participating in the slave trade, they often tried to avert the ill-effects of the trade. This trade brought in exchange, *inter alia*, fire arms, gun-powder, tobacco and rum, all calculated, under Ghanaian conditions, to debase the society and ruin the economy. So at an early period, African merchants, particularly those in non-auriferous regions like the Slave Coast, sought to limit these dangerous imports by demanding part payment for slaves in gold, which the Portuguese then brought in from Brazil. In the 18th century, the English Royal African Company went further east along the coast to Whydah and Sao Thome to purchase gold and was tempted under African pressure to exchange it for slaves. But the company directors sternly forbade such a transaction, insisting on Africans accepting English manufactures.[13]

Also the Asante policy of not enslaving Asante citizens tended to prevent the physical collapse of the kingdom. Instead of depleting its labour force, the Asante government by resorting to external slaving activities rather added to its labour force by bringing in captives from neighbouring countries. In the same vein, the Akan generally resented the intrusion of foreign cultures like those of Islam from the north. Akan culture was impregnable as long as its underlying economy remained strong. It took Europeans several centuries to penetrate the Ghanaian interior precisely because of this. But when the Atlantic Slave Trade finally weakened Ghana's economy, Ghanaian culture could no longer hold foreign European culture at bay as was the case with northern Islamic intrusion earlier. Indeed, the change was so dramatic that the Akan states that had earlier rejected Islam, finally accepted "everything" European, rejecting "everything" African.[14]

The slave trade also destroyed factors providing stimulus to growth in Ghana. We have already discussed a number of factors i.e. iron-smelting, gold mining and agriculture. Others were the Arab trade from the north, and the 16th and 17th century Atlantic trade from the European trading posts in the south. Traffic from either direction led to increased economic activities. Together with other factors, these led to population growth, political cohesion, enhanced agriculture and commercial activities. Because the slave trade was late in coming to Ghana the country sprang into a lead in West Africa, as other countries in the sub-region had these early development traits jeopardized by the early Atlantic Slave Trade within their borders. However, when the slave trade finally tightened its grip on Ghana, all these advantages disappeared and decline set in. The trade corrupted the traditional rulers and elite. It is important to stress that the slave trade brought decline through the destruction of labour and skill. So in traditional states like Asante with the policy of preventing internal slave raiding and rather bringing in captives from outside, the labour force was preserved and no decline was experienced. But in others like Akwamu which indulged in internal slave raiding, decline was absolute.

NOTES

1. Rodney, Walter 1969. *Op. cit.*
2. Kea, R. A. 1969. Akwamu-Anlo relations, c.1750–1813. *Transactions of the Historical Society of Ghana* x: 29–63.
3. Rodney, Walter 1969. *Op. cit.*
4. *Ibid.*
5. Swanzy, Henry 1956. A trading family in the nineteenth century Gold Coast. *Transactions of the Gold Coast and Togoland Historical Society* II (ii): 87–120
6. Rouch, Jean 1955. *Op cit.*
7. Kea, R. A. 1970. Osei Kwame's interdiction on Danish trade 1788–90. *Ghana Notes and Queries* 11: 36–41.
8. *Ibid.*
9. *Ibid.*
10. Penford, D. A. 1971. *Op. cit.*
11. Rodney, Walter 1969. *Op. cit.*
12. La Anyane, S. 1963. *Op. cit.*, p. 10.
13. Rodney, Walter 1969. *Op. cit.*
14. Rouch, Jean 1955. *Op. cit.*

Chapter 4

THE OIL PALM ERA

General
So far we have seen how during the gold era, Ghana's economy took off, and development started in all sectors. We have also discussed how in the 18th century the slave trade brought a serious set back when both agricultural and manufacturing industrial bases established during the gold era were now weakened.

With the collapse of this first effort, the only way to resume the path to economic growth was to find another booster in place of gold. In the 19th century, it was obvious that this would have to be a number of agricultural products, which when fully developed would help to foster international trade favourable to Ghana. This trade would, in turn, provide capital for extractive and manufacturing industrial growth.

Although the 19th century has gone down into history as the revolutionary years, economic recovery eluded Ghana. This was because agriculture which could have proved a booster did not go well. Besides, trade, not only because of poor agriculture, but also because of other factors as well, could not produce the required capital for manufacturing industrial growth. Indeed, the tragedy of the 20th century has its roots in the 19th century. This century more or less coincided with the oil palm era.

We have already referred to extractive and manufacturing industries. The other type of industry we shall be concerned with in this work is agricultural industry or the activity of growing and harvesting crops, fishing and livestock keeping. In this chapter, we shall discuss cultivation and harvesting of a number of crops, the most important being the oil palm.

Origins and Early Development of Oil Palm
There is a controversy about the original home of the oil palm. While some scholars maintain that the oil palm tree is indigenous to West Africa, others postulate a South American origin. Arguments for a West African origin appear more convincing, particularly since the crop was already well-established in West Africa when the earliest visitors to the West Coast appeared. The plant has from time immemorial been wild and up till now total cultivation has not been achieved. Indeed, a large proportion of

the harvest in Ghana is still from wild groves.

Consequently, the early oil palm industry, which probably dates back to Neolithic times, consisted merely of picking the fruits from wild palm groves and extracting oil from the pericarp. The oil was in the early days turned fully to domestic use, principally as food but also as fuel for oil lamps and pomade for the skin. The palm branches were used as building material. The shell of the kernel was used by blacksmiths for various purposes including iron smelting and the making of gun powder. The kernel itself provided a nutritious oil for home consumption, but this has never been popular. Palm wine tapping is also an ancient occupation which, however, tended to destroy the palm trees.

The 19th Century Agricultural Setting

The 19th century saw significant changes in the industry which now had to cater for the international market and not solely for local consumption as before. By 1820, foreign trade in oil palm products had begun, even though this was on a small scale.[1] The importance of the oil palm industry is best seen in the total 19th century agricultural setting of the country. Generally, Ghana's agriculture in the 19th century is to be considered the country's chief industry. The predominance of primary production simply meant predominance of agriculture, other industries having suffered serious decline.

Agricultural activity, apart from oil palm industry, included growing of corn, groundnuts, mallaguetta pepper, collection of gum copal and tapping of wild rubber.[2] In addition to the above, other food crops were cultivated, mainly cassava, plantains, yams, cocoyams etc. The agricultural technique was simply that of shifting cultivation, or leaving a piece of land fallow for years to regain soil fertility.

In spite of this varied agricultural activity, some scholars maintain that agriculture was in a poor state by the middle of the 19th century, supposedly because farm work was regarded as work for slaves.[3] But as has been seen, Ghana had by the 18th century achieved labour specialization and this included agricultural labouring class, employable for farm work. In actual fact, the 19th century witnessed several attempts at agricultural improvement but effects of events of the recent past continued to interfere with these developments. The slave trade did not, of course, end with the 18th century and its effects on agriculture persisted in the 19th century. The slave trade caused a lot of rivalry which in the 19th century continued to disturb and unsettle farming,[4] partly through the reduction of agricultural labouring classes. Furthermore, the growing European technological control checked agricultural growth. Gold rush in the 1880s in the Western Region, for instance, affected availability of agricultural labour,[5] but these events did not actually cripple agriculture and the gold rush with its adverse effects on agriculture was only in the western districts.

In the eastern districts, apart from the absence of a gold rush, there were several mountainous areas which were free from inter-ethnic raids of this time and agricultural development was spectacular in these areas. People moved thither for peace and agricultural prosperity. Most of the new arrivals were from the Central Region, already equipped with basic agricultural techniques.

These techniques underwent improvement when, since 1843, missionaries led by the Basel Mission introduced new ideas and methods. From the middle of the 19th century, 1856 precisely, the Basel Mission opened agricultural stations near some of their mission houses for experimentation and extension of agriculture.[6] Encouragement for the community came from a number of private European gardens like Buelah in Cape Coast belonging to Rev. T. B. Freeman. These were vegetable and orchard gardens, and Eastern Region had several. The Region also witnessed the establishment of several government projects to introduce new crops and techniques into the country. The most famous agricultural station opened by government was the Aburi Botanical Gardens in 1890. There, considerable work was done on cocoa. So the Eastern Region became a cradle of new agricultural techniques in the 19th century. And when internecine feuds came to an end in the early 1890s, a lot of energy was now released for agriculture, and farming groups already armed with relatively new techniques began to move out. First, Akwapim and Krobo farmers from the Eastern Region spread throughout Southern Ghana, taking with them improved farming techniques. Again in Southern Ghana, a number of Asante farming groups, attracted by the new techniques, settled in various villages and helped to improve farming there. In Northern Ghana, it was the Dagombas and Mamprussi who first got hold of agricultural techniques and spread them throughout the Northern Region.[7]

The Role of Oil Palm Industry

This was the situation in general agriculture throughout the country in the 19th century. The areas where oil palm developed were Akwapim and Krobo in the eastern districts and the area behind Saltpond in the Central Region.[8] So even though the oil palm industry existed in many parts of the country it was in the cradle of agricultural development, i.e. the Eastern Region, that this very first major agricultural crop of Ghana developed to supply the international market, while still satisfying growing domestic needs.

As the nineteenth century wore on and the Atlantic slave trade showed signs of crumbling down under international pressure, the palm oil industry (i.e. the collection of palm nuts from wild groves and the preparation of palm products by local farmers) gradually expanded to replace slaving activities. The European traders on the coast, too, turned from the slave trade increasingly to the export of palm products from Ghana and elsewhere in West Africa to satisfy growing demands in the soap and margarine factories of the UK as well as the animal feed-processing plants of Germany where the industrial revolution had undermined the slave trade economy in favour of commodity trade. So the oil palm industry emerged the obvious major activity in the post slave trade era. In the early part of the twentieth century, there were even signs of mechanizing the industry on European-owned plantations and by the use of hand presses, but in this connection, there never was a significant achievement.

In the predominant primary production sector, oil palm products were by far the greatest, accounting in 1881–5 for about 73 per cent of total exports in value (palm oil 47 per cent, palm kernel 26 per cent). It has to be noted, however, that local consumption of palm oil was very high while palm kernels were mainly for export.[9] The international trade in palm products, having started by 1820, became the principal agricultural item of trade in the country from 1850 onwards. Oil palm products for export reached a peak in 1884, when some 20,000 tonnes of palm oil and 40,000 tonnes of palm kernels were exported.[10]

Decline of the Oil Palm Industry

A war-mongering capitalist world, however, exploded in 1914 and caused considerable harm to growing but fragile economies of West Africa. In Ghana, the 19th century oil palm industry had a shaky foundation. Only very few palm trees were actually cultivated; the vast majority of oil palm products, as has been seen earlier in this chapter, came from wild groves and in fact, even in the 20th century, the industry still consisted mainly of picking the nuts and preparing palm oil and kernels by traditional methods for export. Such an industry, without a strong agricultural practice, could not withstand the storm of a world war.

It was German firms in West African territories which, throughout the 19th and early twentieth century, purchased and shipped a large proportion of palm produce in the country. The First World War caused the closure of all these German firms and the export prices of the West African oil palm produce consequently fell from £15 to £8 per tonne from 1912 to 1916. Furthermore, it was German farmers who used palm kernel cake as animal feed; British farmers did not, and therefore, could not sustain demand for this product after the departure of the Germans from Africa. Even more important was the fact that there were no mills in the United Kingdom for palm kernels as in Germany. Finally, there was a growing shortage of tonnage from West Africa to the United Kingdom due to the exigencies of war 1914–18. After the war, demand for oil palm products increased, but the nature of these demands were such that only countries such as Malaya that had mechanized the oil palm industry could meet them. Ghana's industry remained one of merely picking nuts and using traditional methods of oil extraction; and so the industry declined.[11]

Cotton

The origins of cotton cultivation have been briefly discussed in Chapter 2. It has been shown that the industry is very ancient and its importance even at the very early stages must be appreciated. Efforts towards cotton development in the 19th century were typical of the century, in that they were reminiscent of 19th century revolutionary trends and yet at the same time scanty in results, because of tremendous obstacles to development. This left cotton development an average achievement by the turn of the century.

First, in the area of production, considerable changes were expected. The early cotton growing and manufacturing industry was widespread; involving almost every household which locally produced, spun and wove the cotton into cloth for its members. Gradually in the 19th century, this picture of a household cotton industry was changing to one of communal cotton production. This assumed appreciable proportions by the middle of the 19th century. There was enlarged community farming to support the cotton export needs of Ghana. In addition, a number of cotton plantations sprang up to make cotton the second most important commercial crop of Ghana during the third quarter of the century.[1][2]

As has been seen, cotton cultivation was first established in the Alavanyo district of the Volta Region, Northern Ghana and in the Bonwire area of Asante. By the turn of the 19th century, the area most devoted to cotton cultivation in the Volta Region was Krepi; west of the Volta it was Krobo first, then Akwapem. The most suitable cotton market was the Krobo town of Akuse on the Lower Volta. Krobo and Akwapem farmers were, of course, close to this market and this gave them an advantage over Krepi farmers, who had to pay exorbitant transport costs to bring cotton to Akuse. So here again, Krobo and Akwapem led the entire country in cotton production. Many other areas continued under cotton with production ranging from average to low.

The early cotton industry was on individual basis at the community and household levels. The changes in the 19th century included a change in the agents promoting cultivation of the crop. Activities continued on community and household farms but now missionaries and government officials joined in the effort to develop cotton in Ghana. The body most concerned with the scientific development of the industry was the British Cotton Growing Association which arrived in Ghana towards the end of the 19th century.

The activities of the British Cotton Growing Association included encouraging farmers by supplying them with cotton seeds. This, at the same time, involved improving techniques, as new varieties of cotton were introduced by the Association. Improved strains which could withstand tropical diseases were also distributed to farmers particularly at Anum and Labolabo in Krepi.

Few cotton plantations were established by the Mission Stations as experimental farms and a few more by the British Cotton Growing Association or private individual European gardeners. Small ginneries were also established in other cotton growing centres in the North.[13]

These 19th century efforts to change cotton cultivation did not bear much fruit. Obstacles to cotton development included the incidence of insect pests and other plant diseases. By 1870, these had discouraged plantation effort, causing considerable decline in their development. Increases in cotton exports at the beginning of the 20th century were, therefore, only moderate. In 1904, 519 bales were exported; in 1906, it rose to 857. But twenty years later the figure was 886 bales, a clear sign of stagnation, though the export figure is no true indication of a successful crop development. Household cotton industry (cultivation, spinning and weaving by members of the household), once widespread, now witnessed a sharp decline, partly because of agronomy reasons, and partly because export of raw cotton affected it, as did the import of cheap European or Japanese finished cotton goods. Interest in the cotton industry waned, some of it going to other field crops, particularly groundnuts.

Rubber
The rubber industry has a very long history behind it. Like that of several other tropical tree crops its origin lies in a very dim and ancient past. In Ghana, when this tree was first identified by about the 17th century as a useful plant, it was in a wild state as part of the evergreen tropical forest. Only forest belts with generous rainfall patterns supported rubber in this wild habitat. Consequently, rubber trees were in abundance in the high rainfall zone of south western Ghana and in the relatively wet high forest region of Asante.

Wild rubber collected from the forest played an important role in the early village economy of Ghana, as it was put to various domestic and industrial uses. Its 17th and 18th century use was many sided and constituted a boom to the rubber collecting industry in particular and a blessing to cottage manufacturing industry as a whole. Although Ghana could then not refine rubber for sophisticated and extended uses, the product in its raw state served the rural community well. When tapped from the wild tree, rubber yielded a gum-like substance to seal broken calabashes, leaking canoes, and all kinds of earthenware and wooden receptacles for both domestic and industrial uses.

In the 19th century, the industry entered a new phase. Throughout the first half of the 19th century, the traditional uses of rubber declined with the increase in European imported goods. At the same time, exports of crude rubber to Europe began. The earliest record of rubber export reveals a mere moderate achievement but the invention in Europe of the pneumatic tyre towards the end of the 19th century blew out the demand for rubber out of all proportion to the peasant supply of the product. This created a steep export price of rubber. Accordingly, a number of European-owned rubber plantations sprang up to meet this demand, and take advantage of rising rubber prices. European nationals were able to apply the high standard of technique needed on rubber plantations. The rise in rubber production in Ghana was very rapid. The export figures reflected this rapid growth. In 1880, only 0.05 tonne of rubber was exported. Six years later in 1886, 691.57 tonnes were exported.[14] Indeed, in another six years, rubber excelled oil palm products to rank first on the country's agricultural export list.[15] Ghana became the world's third largest rubber exporter.

The glorious days of rubber in Ghana were, however, short lived. This was due to several reasons. There was the old 19th century problem of peasant collection of wild crops, in this case rubber, in stead of cultivating them and here the reason for decline was the failure to improve upon this position as demanded by the times. In stead of taking to new cultivation techniques of rubber, the peasants were rendered mere spectators of European skill and performance, too complicated and expensive for them to acquire. So naturally, they became disinterested in rubber, causing decline even in the wild rubber collection sector. They shifted to other crops, like cocoa, which demanded less expensive and complex techniques. So the meteoric rise of rubber was due mainly to the European plantations which in the social and political climate of Ghana, could not ensure a prolonged success.

At the turn of the 19th century, rubber, like oil palm industry, needed improved techniques to survive. But for this improved plantation rubber to be established it must fetch a good price as it had done in the 1880s. But the 20th century opened with wide fluctuations in the price of plantation rubber on the English market. The price dropped sharply and this low price could not support the expensive agricultural techniques required in the production of plantation rubber. As indicated, the former alternative (wild rubber) could not compete with plantation rubber in the modern world. In any case peasant wild rubber exports had already declined in Ghana, hence the rubber industry was bound to collapse in the early part of this century.[16]

Coffee

The 19th century revolution in different aspects of Ghanaian national life included the introduction of cash crops and the relevant agricultural techniques for their development. In some cases, development of the crops involved only an improvement upon an already on going process. That happened with crops like oil palm and rubber with which peasant farmers had been familiar from time immemorial and which might have even been indigenous. In other cases, it was a matter of first time cultivation in Ghana following the introduction of the crop in the 19th century, mostly by missionaries. Such crops included cocoa and coffee.[17]
In all cases except cocoa, which belonged more to the 20th century than to the 19th century, there were very serious ups and downs. Coffee more than any other crop had a very difficult start and was still not well established by the outbreak of the First World War.

Before the mid 19th century, the Basel Mission had introduced coffee plantations in some of their mission stations, notably Akwapem. This was yet another opportunity for Akwapem farmers to excel. It was indeed Akwapem farmers who, in spite of difficulties, persevered with the cultivation of coffee and kept up the industry through thick and thin during the two decades after 1870.

It was the adoption of new techniques that aided the local farmers in their struggle to develop coffee. Coffee has a number of varieties and with the help of the missionaries, who made these varieties available, the peasant farmers turned to new varieties more resistant to disease. By 1880s, therefore, Akwapem farmers had established small but fairly prosperous individual coffee plantations throughout the region. Demand for coffee was, of course, more elastic than for cocoa, which, unlike coffee, yielded largely luxury products such as chocolate; and when the 1914 war caused a decline in the demand for cocoa, interest in coffee increased.

But the efforts to develop coffee were not fully rewarded. The year 1869 witnessed extensive Asante raids both east and west of the Volta destroying all farm enterprises before them. This seriously affected coffee development projects which were just then coming up. Also, in Akwapim, the area with the greatest interest in coffee growing, borer attack on the coffee crop proved damaging. Attempts to control these pests with the use of chemicals failed. The local farmers got discouraged particularly when advised to cut out affected plants as the only solution available. Coffee exports to Germany thus remained low and the increased production expected by the initially hardworking farmers never came.[18]

Trade

Local and International Trade
Internal trade in any country generates wealth but it is international trade which brings in the largest fortune. In 19th century Ghana, exports were raw materials meant for European manufacturers. They included gold dust, ivory, palm oil, corn, groundnuts, malaguetta pepper, and gum copal. Imports into Ghana were cotton goods, silks, velvets, spirits, wines, tobacco, iron, brass, lead, copper, hardware, cutlery, gun powder, cowries, tea, sugar and beer. These were all finished European goods. Of the exports, agricultural produce formed the greater part.

Local trade, i.e. where trade items were locally produced, distributed and consumed, was also important for the growing economy. Items of local trade were mainly food stuffs. They were root crops and a number of grains. Local trade also patronized handicrafts.

Local and international trade were fully integrated; very often, the same trader specializing in the distribution of locally-produced crafts and food stuffs would also add trade in some of the imported items. Petty traders in food stuffs often operated just within particular localities, but those who combined distribution of local food stuffs with that of imported European goods tended to go over longer distances and indeed qualified as long-distance traders.

The currency used in international trade was normally the same as in local trade. However, there was more barter in local trade than international trade. Throughout the 19th century, the currencies in circulation during the 18th century were still there, but increasingly they were being replaced by both British and United States silver coins. Similarly, the trade routes for both local and international trade were sometimes integrated.

Roads

The "great roads" carrying the north-south traffic[19] served the international trade more or less exclusively. This was because the goods carried from the interior to the sea coast were nearly all meant for the Atlantic trade. It was along these same routes that imported items travelled into the interior.

A second category of roads ran in more or less the same north-south direction but for shorter distances than the great roads. They served the early local traffic involving exchange of coastal produce such as fish and salt on one hand and forest products, especially food stuff, on the other. At the same time, the northern termini of such routes served areas with export crops carried south by the local trader after disposing off his fish and salt.

A third category of roads was the coastwise traffic which involved trafficking in goods in both east and west directions along the coast. At times, the second and third categories of trade routes were linked by minor routes tending to create a network of the minor routes all over what is now southern Ghana. A number of small trading centres existed on the coast, apart from the major ones.

Trade Routes

The following were the categories of trade routes (Fig. 3). The first category was basically what we described under the slave trade era but it developed minor changes and needs to be discussed again. It consisted as before of four trade paths, serving the international trade between the coast and the Asante interior. There was one route in the far west of Ghana coming from Kumasi through

48   An Economic History of Ghana

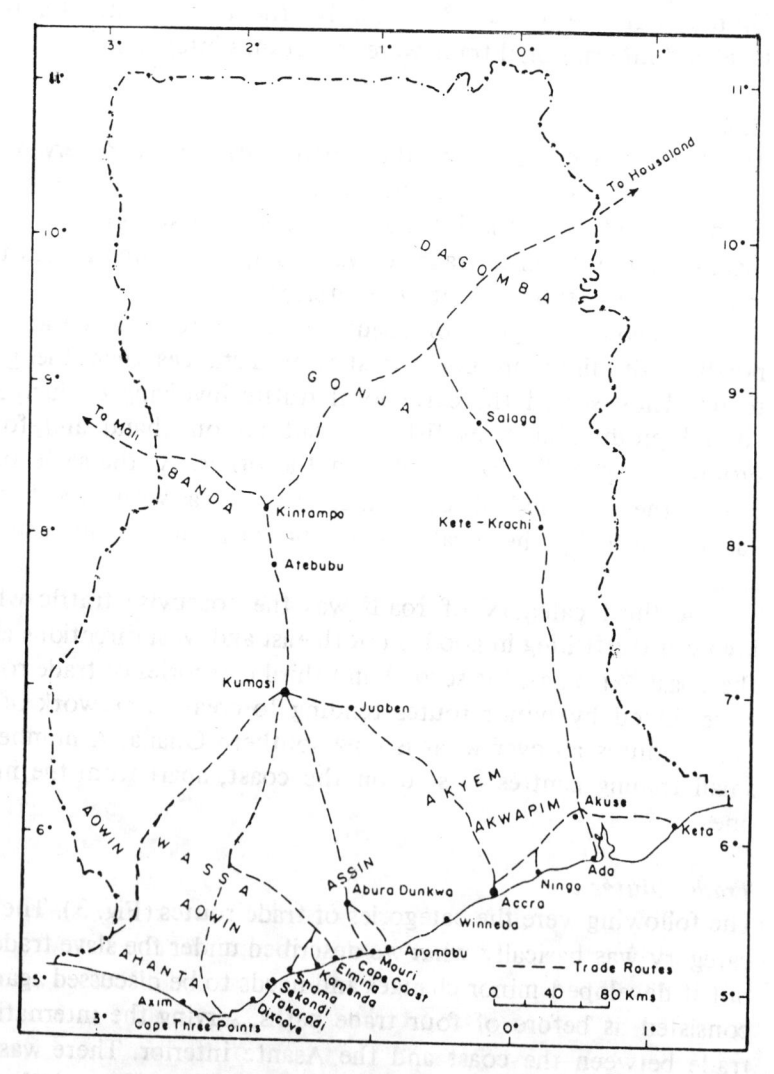

Fig. 3   Ghana Trade Routes in the 19th Century

Aowin, passing through the Ahanta country in south-western Ghana to Cote d'Ivoire. The next route was from Kumasi through Wassaw where it divided into two, the eastward branch going to Elmina, Komenda and Shama and the western branch went through Axim District to Cape Three Points and a few neighbouring ports. The central trade route went from Kumasi to the Assin country and then to Abura Dunkwa, where it divided into two, one branch going to Anomabu and the other to Mouri and Cape Coast. The eastern route passed through Juaben, Akyem, Akwapem to Accra. To these we must add a Volta route which reached northern Ghana without passing through Asante jurisdiction.

The second category of trade routes originated from a number of trading centres on the sea coast. They included Keta, Ada, Ningo, Accra, Winneba, Saltpond, Cape Coast, Elmina, Komenda, Sekondi, Dixcove and Axim. In some cases, parts of the trade routes followed the courses of some notable rivers like the Volta, Ankobra and Tano, into the interior. An example in 1877 of a trade route in this category started from Ada, where the trader procured fish, to Krepi, where, after selling the fish, he collected canoe loads of palm kernel. He stopped at Kpong and Amedeka, the port of Akuse, and sold all the kernels, thus feeding the southern traffic of the international trade. It was here also that he further participated in the foreign trade by buying some imported items, including tobacco and cloth, with which he returned to Ada for the retail trade.[20]

Another route in the second category was the Cape Coast-Foso road which was actually part of the great central north-south road. But the southern end of it swarmed with Fanti traders who used it as part of a net-work of local trade routes. Thus, there were offshoots of trade paths from this trunk road to the east and west linking villages and hamlets with this great artery of international trade. It was by this means that imported goods got distributed at the grass-root level in south-central Ghana. Based on the Keta lagoon was yet another type of trade routes utilizing the lagoon to ferry goods from the sea-shore into the hinterland. These goods were often smuggled across the eastern border into Ghana in demi-Johns and the smugglers used the lagoon to escape from Ghana customs officials. Extensions of this route reached Krepi on the left bank of the Volta and Kwahu on the right. The Kwahu route had to pass through Krobo which was at times so turbulent, particularly during the slave trade days, that it had to be frequently abandoned.

There were coastwise routes which were used for the exchange of both local trade goods and for the disposal of imported items. A trader starting from Cape Coast could carry tobacco and rum and sell those along his coastal route to Axim. But before reaching Axim he would have acquired local trade goods like agricultural produce which he would dispose off before returning to Cape Coast.

As already indicated, the trans-Saharan southbound traffic created two important termini in Ghana at Salaga and Kintampo, which it fed with items like Moroccan leather and other manufactured goods from North Africa as well as livestock, particularly, sheep and goats. From Salaga and Kintampo these items reached Asante to join the central-southern traffic to the sea coast. In Asante, a number of minor trade paths led to Kumasi and Juaben as collecting centres for kola nuts which were then transmitted to the two northern emporia for the return journey of the Saharan traders. One batch of the latter left Ghana through Gyaman on a north-westerly route towards Jenne and Timbuktu, and another through the north-eastern corner of Ghana towards Kano in Nigeria. Another route which traversed the north-eastern section of Ghana completely outside Asante domain swammed with traders going up the Volta river from the south with imported western manufactured goods meant for distribution both along the river and in the north, and returning down the Volta with goats and sheep procured at Salaga. At various stops on the river, local traders emerged through numerous minor trade routes to procure trade goods for distribution in the riverine states on both sides of the Volta.

Transportation

We have considered trade routes in Ghana during the 19th century. Essentially, they were foot-paths through forest, woodland and grassland which during the rainy season were mostly overgrown with bush and were at times impassable. Headloading was the only means of transport that could be used on them. In our present discussion transportation means improvements on these routes or foot-paths for easy movement of goods and people.

The history of transportation in Ghana epitomizes the

economic underdevelopment of the country in the 19th century. The development of transportation like that of mining etc. required considerable technological experience, but the growth of the latter had been disrupted in 18th century Ghana. European companies and administration employed some technology in Ghana but for furthering their own aims, quite different from Ghanaian aspirations. With regards to roads, the few they built or caused to be built in the 19th century were meant to provide them with security and further their economic exploitative activities. So transportation in 19th century Ghana had poor facilities.

When the roads came to be built, some followed notable trade routes like the north-south trunk roads and even the coastwise traffic. The earliest road building efforts were made by the Basel Mission, which wanted to link its two main stations at Christiansborg and Akropong with a road system good enough for bullock carts. In this way, they could cart supplies arriving at Accra from Germany to this hill station with ideal weather conditions for European habitation. They had considerable problems as the road went through tsetse-infested forests and the entire Ghanaian environment was unsuitable for beasts of burden. However, the Mission's road through Aburi reached Akropong by the 1860s and even the Government extended it through Odumasi to Kpong on the Volta soon afterwards. This road served several interests: first, the Government, whose officials preferred the cool hill climate of Aburi to the hot plains of Accra; the Basel set-up which fostered both gospel and trade, and finally the purely commercial sector, with wider interests linking the port of Accra to the trading business on the Lower and Middle Volta as far north as Kete-Krachi and Salaga. Geographically, the road was well placed to serve these interests, but its construction did not come with all the benefits expected. There were no carriages to be used and headloading continued. Hand carts and cask rolling in the immediate vicinity of company depots provided no useful substitute for animal-drawn long-distance carts. Consequently, the Government had no incentive in devoting resources to building more roads. It decided to continue in the old practice of getting the chiefs to mobilize labour force to clear the existing path ways of bush, particularly during the rainy season. As the Government failed to pay the chiefs on time, the work of clearing the paths was not done well. A few examples of monies spent on road maintenance follow: in 1881, the total amount spent was £888; in 1882, £1,446; in 1883, £1,501; in 1884 £3,998 and in 1885 £3,353. Even in the Tarkwa area where the chiefs were to clear the roads because they were already benefiting from mineral proceeds, and the Government and mine owners because of the obvious advantages of mineral exploitation, not much was done as what was everybody's business turned out to be nobody's business.[21]

The disincentive in building roads without carriages to use them crystalized into some desire for developing instead water transport for which steam launches were already available in the country, having been introduced into West African exploration as early as 1830s on the Niger and 1850s on the Volta. Thus, on the Volta in the 1880s, Miller Brothers, Basel Mission and Swanzy as well as the local British Government operated steam launches between Amedeka and Ada. On the Ankobra, a mining company operated a steam launch mainly to help bring up the river mining machinery and stores from Axim. The rest of the journey from the river to Tarkwa was by bush road. Canoe traffic by the local people from Assini up the river Tano was also highly developed. Early plans for building railways to link Elmina and Kumasi, and secondly the mining area of Tarkwa with the coast remained on paper.[22]

With all these problems of developing road transportation, Ghana never achieved much by way of good roads in the 19th century. Thus, the only roads worth the name were first the Accra-Kpong road, the military road from Cape Coast to Prasu built by Sir Garnet Wolsely in 1874 for moving troops against Asante; a short stretch from Cape Coast to Elmina and the road from Shama to Tarkwa.

Generally, therefore, road transportation was poor in 19th century Ghana and this naturally affected trade. There was the difficulty of retailing trade imports and of collecting agricultural produce at the ports for export. What was even worse was the obstacle in the way of exchange of agricultural produce locally and the resultant high percentage of spoilage certainly discouraged farmers.

Crafts, Extractive and Manufacturing Industries

Crafts and industries, both manufacturing and extractive, also reflected the nature of the 19th century ailing economy. The growth of manufacturing industries depended, among other things, on the rigorous application of technology to traditional crafts, but local technological development was stagnant and 19th century manufacturing industries did not benefit much from European technological innovations, the latter having been confined to the few non-traditional crafts coming up about the second quarter of the century.

The traditional crafts and manufacturing industries which had been in practice since time immemorial and which continued into the 19th century included pottery, textiles, metal and leather works, boat-building and oil processing.

The metal workers were mainly blacksmiths and goldsmiths using age-old traditional methods to produce a number of items. The blacksmiths, using iron, made hoes and cutlasses and forged spears and arrows for hunting. They also repaired guns and did minor works in other metals. The goldsmiths produced gold rings, chains and brooches. In gold-smithery the 19th century standard was said to be very high. This was the case with pottery too. With textiles went dyeing; oil processing continued into the 19th century, even though there were no improvements in the techniques applied.

The second category of manufacturing industries were European-introduced crafts including carpentry, joinery, cask-making and lock-making. These came to supplement traditional wood works like carving which had existed before the 19th century. It was the Basel Mission in particualr that introduced most of these new wood crafts in connection with their work. They needed masonry, carpentry and joinery as well as lock-making to help in the erection of structures in their emerging mission stations, and they thought it fit to train their own tradesmen and craftsmen in these areas. So came into existence all over the country, masons, carpenters, locksmiths etc. who were later to play such an important role in the furniture and construction business in Ghana. Cask-makers also provided a vital service to the trading community; since 1890, unitl the coming of vehicular transport, cask-rolling, was the chief, if not the only, means of transporting palm oil, not only in the immediate vicinity of the trading depots, but also over longer distances from the interior to the coast.

The standard of manufacturing industries in the 19th century was low. Mostly only simple technology was applied to these processes. There was a complete lack of enterprise. Even the labour supply which should have been specialized for the purpose was totally inadequate. The result of these manufacturing industrial efforts was, therefore, unimpressive. So on the whole, we could assert that manufacturing industries played a relatively minor role in the economy of 19th century Ghana.

The decline of the extractive industries has also been noted.[23] What happened in the 19th century was that these industries which dragged on their existence till then, and in a few cases even achieved some progress within their mitigated circumstances, now received their death blows and more or less went into extinction.

The 19th century was, indeed, a test period when new technology was needed to overcome obstacles in the way of further mining ventures. It was significant, for instance, that the African gold miners at Tarkwa, from 1877 onwards, struggled in vain to get help from Pierre Bonnat who had arrived with water pumps suitable for their flooded gold pits (90 metres down). Their helplessness in watching their age-long pits gradually reach the water table and consequently get flooded and Bonnat's refusal to lend them his water pumping equipment, which he used later to resuscitate their abandoned pits for himself,[24] sums up the history of Ghana's economic tragedy. It marks the end of an era. It is true that the gold era had ended in the 17th century, but not African efforts to use gold as a lever to economic progress. Reduced local technical achievements, due to the slave trade, weakened these efforts all along. The 19th century was the turning point when the local miners hoped to use the newly European-imported technology to achieve a break-through. But Bonnat's action in turning down the requests of the anxious Ghanaian miners epitomizes the Afro-European economic drama. The possibility of a breakthrough was firmly ruled out by the European take-over of the precious metals in Ghana's soil. The 19th century did not start Ghana's doom but it sealed it.

NOTES

1. **La Anyane, S. 1963.** *Ghana Agiculture. Its Economic Development*

from Early Times to the Middle of the Twentieth Century, p. 31. London: Oxford University Press.
2. Bevin, H. J. 1956. The Gold Coast economy about 1880. *Transactions of the Gold Coast and Togoland Historical Society* II (ii): 73—86.
3. Dickson, K. B. 1963. Origin of Ghana's Cocoa industry. *Ghana Notes and Queries* 5: 4—9.
4. La Anyane, S. 1963. *Op. cit.*, p. 11.
5. *Ibid.*, p. 15
6. *Ibid.*, p. 14
7. *Ibid.*, p. 11.
8. Bevin, H. J. 1956. *Op. cit.*
9. *Ibid.*
10. La Anyane, S. 1963. *Op. cit.*, p. 31.
11. *Ibid.*, pp. 34—36; Bevin, H. J. 1956. *Op. cit.*
12. La Anyane, S. 1963. *Op. cit.*, p. 50
13. *Ibid.*
14. *Ibid.*, p. 46.
15. Dickson, K. B. 1963. *Op. cit.*
16. La Anyane, S. 1963. *Op. cit.*, pp. 48—49.
17. Experimentation of small coffee gardens around the European forts probably occurred in the 17th and 18th centuries.
18. *See* La Anyane, S. 1963. *Op. cit.*, p. 53.
19. *See* Fig. 3.
20. Bevin, H. J. 1956. *Op. cit.*
21. *Ibid.*
22. *Ibid.*
23. See p.33.
24. Boateng, E. A. 1957. The Tarkwa mining industry — A retrospect. *Bulletin of the Gold Coast Geographical Association*, II (i): 5—9.

Chapter 5

THE COCOA ERA

Political-economic Situation

At the beginning of the 20th century, Ghana had a total land area of 238,000 square kilometres, made up of the 'Colony', Asante and the Northern Territories. Togoland was then not part of Ghana.[1] The population was not much more than a million. Most of these were still living under the influence of their chiefs, but British colonial authority, which often weighed heavily on the communities, was imposed on them.

To understand early 20th century British policy towards Ghana, one has to look at the country's economy then. As already discussed, Ghana entered the 20th century with predominantly primary production and export sectors. It was first hoped that the international trade involved would increase, generate growth in the economy and result in an economic "take-off" in Ghana. That "take-off" should involve acquiring skills which would be applied to the primary products to generate a more balanced economic activity. But it soon became clear that Third World countries like Ghana were unlikely to benefit from international trade in this way, owing to the very nature of their exports.[2] This was so first because of market forces which manipulated Third World exports against their interests and secondly because of the necessity for Britain to follow Bonnat's line of action and establish regulations that worked against African ownership of minerals with more elasticity on the world market as well as prevent African acquisition and application of technology to their raw materials to achieve higher value. With regard to the world market prices of Ghana's exports, they fluctuated violently resulting generally in low producer prices for Ghana's farming population. Meanwhile, through the same raw material exports, Ghana, more than any other British colony, earned dollars which went to close the UK's dollar gap.[3] Indeed, Ghana was a model colony whose dollar credits Britain thriftly harnessed so as to benefit from them. This was sometimes done even at the expense of Ghana itself which was not allowed to import goods from other hard currency areas apart from the UK so as to conserve dollars for Britain.[4]

In the 20th century, British West African policy claims to take cognizance of Lugard's dual mandate — a symbiotic existence for mutual benefits[5] — but this remained a mere slogan when it came to practice. Each country had some peculiarity which would make dual mandate malfunction even if applied genuinely. In the case of Ghana, it was too much of a model colony for the British to sacrifice their advantages for mutual benefits, particularly at times of dollar crisis. So the tendency was more of regarding Ghana as existing for the benefit of the mother country, Britain, than anything else. Britain with her better technological know-how set out to exploit the natural resources of Ghana for the benefit of British manufacturers and industrialists. British colonial power was imposed to support this programme. Anything Ghana gained out of this relationship was indirect and a mere by-product.

Origins of Cocoa Industry
That was the politico-economic situation of Ghana during the cocoa era, the beginnings of which we shall trace back to the late 19th century, and follow its course to the 1980s. The origins of cocoa cultivation actually dates back to early 19th century, but then there was a long gap when no more was heard about cocoa until after the mid-century. As usual it was the enterprising Basel Missionaries who set up in 1857 an experimental farm at Akropong and nursed cocoa seedlings imported from Surinam and distributed them to local farmers in Akwapem and Krobo. Cultivation seems to have ceased again but in 1878 Teteh Quashie, a local blacksmith, brought back from Fernando Po a few pods with which he started a farm at Mampong in Akwapem. He sold the early harvests to local farmers and later in 1885 began exports to Europe. When the Government botanical gardens were established at Aburi in 1890 to, among other things, nurse cocoa seedlings they added to Teteh Quashie's work, accelerating the spread of cocoa cultivation in Akwapem and elsewhere.[6]

The main reasons for this final success in establishing cocoa in the country were the cessation of slave raids and local conflicts in Ghana, which released for agriculture a great deal of energy, formally expended on feuds. Teteh Quashie's experiments matured at the right time and, in the absence of a gold rush in the Eastern Region, unlike the Western Region, they helped to establish a lasting local interest in cocoa cultivation. The government's contribution here through Aburi Botanical Gardens was to provide models of technique which made the industry more efficient and widespread.[7]

The Spread of Cocoa Cultivation
It was only in the late 19th century that cocoa became an important part of the world's economy. In 1893, total world exports of cocoa coming mainly from South America were 77,000 tonnes. This figure rose to 500,000 tonnes in 1925 representing a remarkable increase in cocoa production within a short time. This increase was made possible by the extension of cocoa cultivation from the New World to West Africa, where Ghana was the leading producer for decades. By the time this South American species reached West Africa, the local species as described above had already been established.

In 1905, British and French West Africa contributed only about 1 per cent of the total world exports. But by 1925, Ghana alone contributed nearly 44 per cent, and Ghana and Nigeria together about 52 per cent of total world exports. In 1936–37, British West Africa and French West Africa contributed 66 per cent of total world exports as follows: Ghana 42 per cent, Nigeria 14 per cent, Cote d'Ivoire 7 per cent, French Cameroons 3 per cent.[8]

For Ghana to achieve this feat, considerable effort was needed. At the beginning of the 20th century, Ghana's position, after losing to white capitalists the commodities with more elasticity on the world market (i.e. gold and other minerals), was precarious. Primary agricultural products whose prices fluctuated violently on the world market gave Ghana no hope of an economic breakthrough. But of course the people, not knowing much about the mechanism of the world market, simply continued to struggle to make the most of agricultural produce.

Apart from fluctuating producer prices, the other serious constraint on agriculture generating enough capital for an economic take-off was the nature of West African agriculture itself, being mainly small peasant holdings, inefficient and incapable of large-scale-production for capital generation. The 20th century tried to rectify this by resorting to rural capitalism, which involved introduction of freehold land ownership and the operation of the market principle as well as the development of an economically-dominant group of large successful peasant farmers. This attempt to solve an old problem of tropical agriculture (i.e. small peasant holdings instead of large estates) was very apt. The credit must go partly to some far-seeing chiefs in the Eastern Region who were willing to sell portions of their lands for individual uses instead of the traditional communal uses with all their constraints on agricultural expansion.[9] With larger estates, capitalization became a lot easier. These were not just large-scale farmers, but also rural creditors, ready to finance the small-scale farmers. A few food and oil palm farmers had saved money from oil palm proceeds for the original injection of finance into the new cocoa industry. There were others involved in the cocoa industry, and these were brokers, factors and clerks operating between the producers and the European firms.[10]

The problem whereby profits from tropical agriculture did not accrue to the primary producers arose partly out of the relationship between the producers and these intermediaries — the brokers, factors and clerks — who bought the produce off the farmers and sold them to the expatriate firms. The 20th century development in Ghana took care of this. The relationship between brokers and farmers came to be very close. There were numerous buying associations and firms which were run by the farmers themselves. Indeed, many of the rich farmers acted as brokers in their own right. In these days, Ghana's cocoa farmers made a good start towards benefiting fully from their entry into world trade.

The actual technique of expanding cocoa cultivation was described as 'migration by company', evolved by the Krobo people as a means of penetrating forest country in the oil palm era.[11] We have discussed the rapid development of agriculture in the Krobo area. Farmers in this rather small flat country had to look elsewhere for more farmlands and this in their geographical situation meant to the west where lies one of West Africa's richest tropical forests in Akyem Abuakwa territory. The strong influence of the co-operative system of the oil palm era and the need for protection against raids in a country not fully rid of slaving activities dictated group, rather than individual, movements into new farming areas. Cocoa farmers from Akwapem and elsewhere copied this Krobo invention in expanding cocoa cultivation into new areas outside their own territories.

After the devastation of the slave trade, useful labour policy once again returned to boost the country's agriculture, particularly in the cocoa-growing areas. In spite of expansion in groups for cocoa farming, cocoa brought an individualistic spirit in production. Most of the cocoa farmers turned into owners and supervisors who employed labour to work on their farms.[12] Naturally, since they were owners, their supervision was so good that labour on the farms became relatively productive yielding, by African standards, very good results.

When we consider the whole cocoa era, reasons for success in cocoa cultivation must include improvement in roads and port facilities for the evacuation of the beans,[13] the formation by government of farmers' co-operatives which removed some traditional obstacles such as lack of farming inputs in the way of cocoa production and the improved world market price in the early 1950s. Details of these will be discussed later in this chapter and the next.

The fact that Ghana, in the first half of the 20th century, excelled in peasant export production in West Africa had been noted. This development of rapid agricultural raw material exports was actually a Third World phenomenon in a number of Asian and African countries. But even in this wider context Ghana's achievement was still unparalleled.[14] Ghana's Eastern Region in 1936–37 produced more cocoa to the acre than almost any other place in the world. In that year, it produced 118,000 tonnes.[15] And the country as a whole exported 317,000 tonnes.[16] During the 1913–35 period, the value of Ghana's cocoa exports increased about 13 times.[17] In 1901, the export value of Ghana's cocoa was £22,000. In 1913, it was £1.5m.[18]

In 1912, the value of Ghana's total trade amounted to £7,448,000. The figure reached £154,663,000 in 1950. In 1951, the cocoa crop alone contributed two-thirds of the total export earnings of Ghana.[19] Put differently, cocoa contributed 50 per cent of the total value of Ghana's exports in 1913, 63 per cent in 1936 and 70 per cent in 1953. The 1936 cocoa exports represented 98 per cent by value of all agricultural exports of the country.[20]

Effects of Cocoa Industry
This rapid expansion of the cocoa industry brought about relatively rapid development in Ghana between the two World Wars.[21] Indeed, Ghana became the most highly developed peasant export

economy in Africa.[22] In specific terms, this meant a number of changes in the country. In the first place, the Ghana Government's finances improved. In 1936, Ghana's revenue from cocoa export tax was £363,000 and duties on imports, most of which were indirectly derived from the cocoa industry, amounted to £2,140,000.[23] But even more important for the future of Ghana was the improvement in the position of the peasant farmers. They became enlightened and ready to defend their rights against the European exporting firms. Their main concern was how to raise the producer price of cocoa. The wealthy farmers had both the understanding of their situation created by the European firms and the money to organize the farmers and others to check the monopoly companies cheating them and tackle the problem of fluctuating world cocoa prices. In effect, an entrepreneurial class had arisen in the cocoa industry, with the ability to organize the people for the welfare of the industry and this involved the control of the market.

Some of the associations formed specifically to seek control over marketing so as to raise producer price of cocoa was the Gold Coast Farmers Association, and the Ashanti Farmers Association Limited (AFA). Numerous farmers associations and companies were also formed both in the colony and in Asante and most of these constituted the African Shippers Union.[24] The Gold Coast Farmers Association was formed in 1919 by an Akwapem farmer, John Ayew, and others. The founders of the AFA were themselves farmers and other workers connected with the cocoa industry. The aim of both these associations and the other companies was to create a "better organization to market our cocoa on a sound basis".[25] To achieve this aim, the associations organized themselves as competitors with the European firms in purchasing cocoa for direct shipment and sale on the European market. The Gold Coast Farmers Association was involved in the 1930–31 cocoa hold-up as a means of forcing the European firms to raise producer prices. The AFA carried out a lot of organizational work. The members had to travel around a lot to explain the Association's aims and policies to the farmers in order to rally support for their activities. These activities constituted a protest against the European firms and they culminated in the second cocoa hold-up in 1937.[26]

The cocoa hold-up of 1937 was organized in the interest of

these local associations seeking to improve the lot of the farmer. The producer price of cocoa had been pushed down by the cocoa "pools" and the 1937 refusal to sell cocoa was aimed at forcing the European firms and the British Colonial Administration to see to raising producer price.

Even by 1942, the struggle to help the Ghanaian farmer continued. In that year, the Agricultural and Commercial Society was trying to use the co-operative movement to achieve what had largely eluded them even after the 1937 cocoa hold-up,[27] namely, higher producer price.

In spite of these efforts to improve Ghana's economy, what the country achieved was just a little more than its low-level food requirements. The rapid development referred to earlier was only in terms of what was exploited, not the benefits to the African producers and it certainly did not reflect on their standard of living. Ghana's peasants might be relatively better off than their counterparts elsewhere in Africa, but their gains were not proportionate to what was expected after such a rapid expansion of the cocoa industry.

That industry, as already indicated earlier in this chapter, was not expected to produce a self-generating economy. But at least it was expected to help develop social services and improve standard of living generally; but even these modest goals were not fully achieved.[28] There were several reasons for this. It has been shown that Ghana depended very heavily on cocoa exports. It was, therefore, exceedingly open to world market forces; and in the circumstances, dependence on the world market price of cocoa, which was subject to extreme fluctuations, was indeed harmful to the country's economy.[29] Around the 1928—30 period, the price of cocoa was so abnormally low that the purchasing power of the people was dramatically reduced.[30] In 1927—28, for instance, the producer price of cocoa ranged from 30 shillings to 24 shillings a load of 30 kilogrammes. During the next two seasons the price dropped to 18 shillings then 16 shillings. In October 1929, a load of cocoa was selling for 9 shillings.[31] In 1930—31, the price of cocoa further went down to 6 shillings and 6 pence per load and one division even reported a price of 2 shillings and 6 pence[32] (see Fig. 4). In 1937, there was yet another heavy fall in the price of cocoa from £45 per tonne at the beginning of 1937/38 season to £25 in December 1937, and finally to £20 in June 1939.[33]

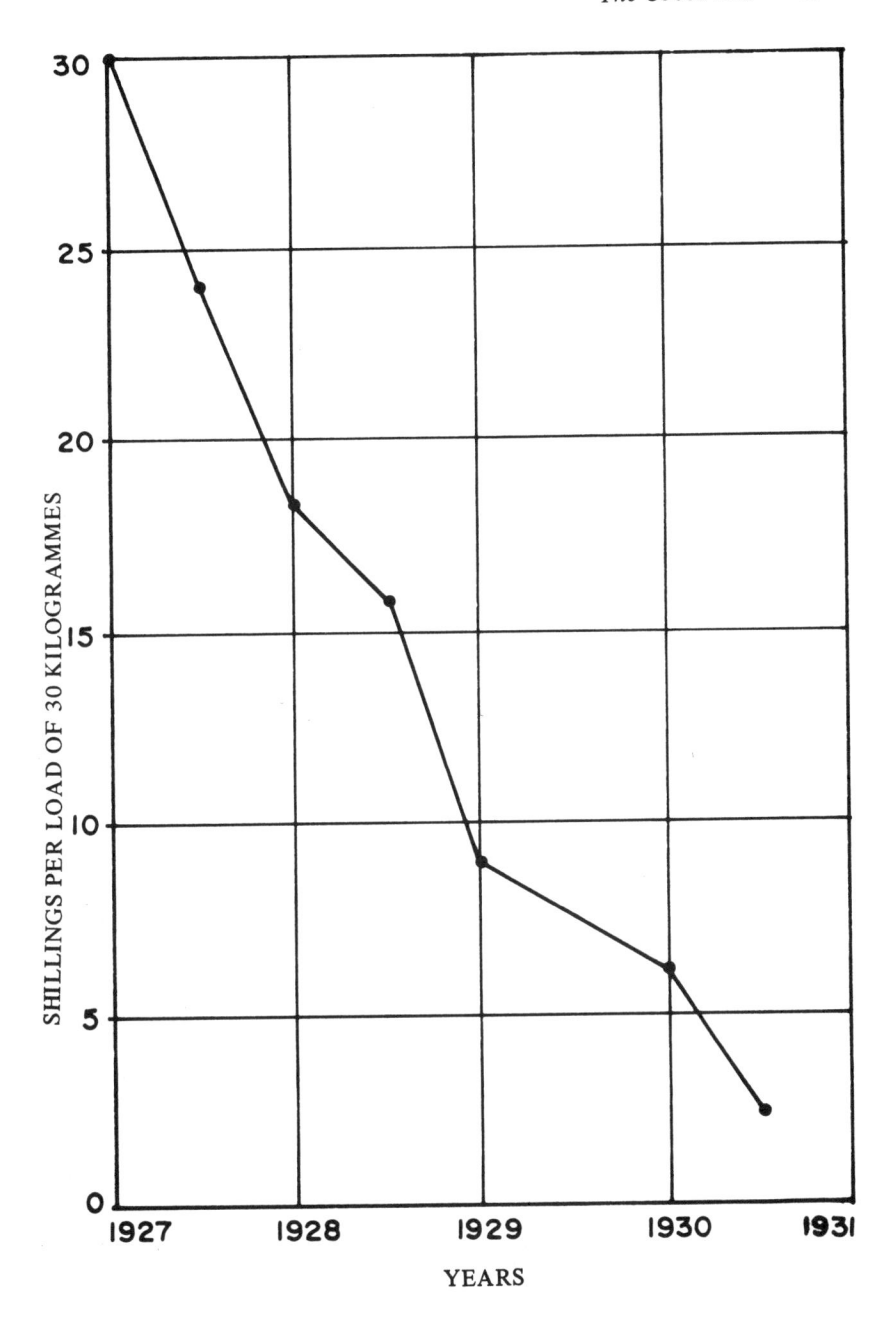

Fig. 4 Fall of Cocoa Producer Prices 1927–30
Source: Computed from Report of the Department of Agriculture 1930–31

We have seen how the African entrepreneurial class and large farmers tried to benefit from international trade and build up local capital. This would have replaced European capital in the cocoa export business. But European capital merged and entrenched itself in Ghana. First, a number of European trading companies merged their interests in 1919 into the African Eastern Trade Corporation (AETC). Speculation in the export trade in 1920-21 was immediately followed by a collapse in cocoa prices, and so there was need for even bigger trading firms and in March 1929 the AETC and the Niger Company were merged into the United Africa Company (UAC). The UAC, in the 1930s, led a new cocoa pool which united all the major buying firms under agreement on buying conditions. In this way, they controlled agricultural produce prices and in fact pushed cocoa prices down[34] as indicated above.

The British Government's reaction to war-time situation was to establish controls in respect of Ghana's agricultural export. In the case of cocoa, these controls had the effect of further reducing the income of the producers and increasing or at least stabilizing the profit margin of the expatriate firms.[35] The immediate post-war period further saw reduction in the earning power of Africans and therefore the prospect of accumulating capital for independent African ventures became even more remote.[36]

These activities thus spelt the doom of the nascent rural bourgeoisie as Sam Rhodie calls the wealthier farmers.[37] They failed to accumulate their own capital to finance the cocoa export business and so control Ghana's international trade for more benefits accruing from this trade.

Alongside the rural 'bourgeoisie', co-operative societies, aimed at improving the quality of cocoa so as to fetch higher prices, sprang up. They succeeded in producing high-quality cocoa through careful harvesting, fermenting and curing of the beans.[38] Even though the rise of these co-operative societies in the 1920s received British Colonial Government support in the 1930s, it did not attain the desired goal of higher cocoa prices.[39] And even though cocoa sold through the co-operative societies commanded a price premium, in practice it made very little difference. Agricultural co-operative societies were expected to finance agriculture and cocoa cultivation in particular.[40] In principle, co-operatives were to tackle agronomic problems but the Ghana co-operatives have never addressed themselves to such problems. The cooperatives could neither finance agriculture nor seek solution to problems of peasant cultivation, even though they first concentrated on post-harvest problems. The persistence of the flat price pool discouraged the co-operatives and they failed to bring about a change in Ghana cocoa culture.

Cocoa Diseases

The foregoing explains, among other things, why the agronomic problems of peasant cultivation did not receive the necessary attention. None of the parties involved in the cocoa industry had time for the peasants' pre-harvest problems on the farms. The smaller peasant farmers were, of course, helpless in every way in face of growing incidence of tropical plant diseases. The British Colonial Administration in Ghana which had direct responsibility in the matter knew about swollen shoot disease in Ghana as early as 1915 but did nothing about it until 1937. The rural bourgeoisie or entrepreneurial class as well as the co-operative societies were aware of cultivation problems since 1930 but they were too absorbed in their struggle with the expatriate firms for higher prices to have time for anything else. Impoverished by events, as shown above, they could not achieve anything, had they the time to tackle agronomic problems of cocoa. These developments culminated in the firm establishment by 1938 of three diseases in the case of cocoa alone, making recovery in the industry later very difficult.

The most damaging of all cocoa diseases was swollen shoot in which a virus carried by mealy bugs attacked the stem causing it to swell and ultimately die. Another disease was caused by capsid attack on the cocoa trees reducing their yield. The third was the pod (particularly black pod) disease which, as the name suggests, affected the cocoa pods. It was a fungal attack on the pod, prevalent in the humid West African climate, increased by bad husbandry, neglect and lack of sanitation on farms.[41]

Significantly, pod diseases occurred at periods of low producer prices when farmers invariably neglected their farms as in 1918 and during the second cocoa price collapse of 1921–22. The other cocoa diseases also first occurred in the 1920s or a little earlier. With regard to swollen shoot disease, the main area of infection lay on the Eastern Region's boundaries with Asante and the Western Region. Then there were scattered isolated outbreaks of swollen shoot in the Eastern Region, Western Region, Asante Region and the Volta Region. In the early 1930s, cocoa farms, situated under the Kwahu scarp in the neighbourhood of Mpraeso, were known to have suffered greatly from black pod disease.[42] Capsid attack took place in many parts of the cocoa-growing area of Ghana.

What aggravated the incidence of cocoa disease was the lateness in tackling them. Since the late 1920s, the Ghana Department of Agriculture carried out sporadic researches into cocoa disease but the information acquired was never put to use and the farms continued to deteriorate. In 1938 when the West African Cocoa Research Institute was established to fulfil a West African need, more systematic research was done but the implementation of their findings by the Colonial Administration in Ghana was again delayed, in some cases, until the 1950s.[43] It was after the Second World War that the Government launched a cocoa rehabilitation programme to tackle cocoa diseases and replace damaged farms with new cocoa plantings. The delay of serious application of government resources to the problem meant that the Government had no solution to the swollen shoot disease by the 1940s and so advised cutting out of infected trees. Extension workers of the Department of Agriculture were to get the farmers to cut out infected trees on their farms. Compulsory cutting out did not work.[44] It was not until early 1950s, after the harm was done, that the West African Cocoa Research Institute came up with a systemic insecticide which when applied to the cocoa tree killed the mealy bug which was the vector of the swollen shoot virus.[45] By 1955, there was some success in capsid control. "Spray-painting" young and medium-sized cocoa warded off capsid attacks of the trees, but mature cocoa could not be so treated, and that year experiments were still going on to see if "Gamelin 20" insecticide could kill the capsid on mature trees. As late as this date, application of copper fungicide to black pod infected cocoa did not work. The Government, in close liaison with the West African Cocoa Research Institute embarked on fertilizer and variety trials. The idea was that the application of some types of fertilizer at various stages of plant growth might produce disease-resistant cocoa trees. The cocoa variety trials concentrated on breeding the most promising types of the Upper Amazon varieties, again with the hope of developing disease-resistant trees.[46]

Cocoa rehabilitation by government was a dismal failure. Late in 1949, it was revealed in the British Parliament that, contrary to the Imperial Government's claim that great progress had been made against swollen shoot in Ghana, "... it is the mealy bug which had made devastating progress".[47] The Government's claim had been made at a London Cocoa Conference, but the conclusions of that Conference actually challenged that claim:

> It is disturbing that so little has been accomplished. We are still only swimming slowly against a strong ebbing tide, which is sweeping the whole industry towards destruction. We concur in the view of the International Commission, which said, in effect: The problem has not received, and is not receiving adequate attention: it must be tackled on a much larger scale.[48]

Facts and figures supported the stand taken by the conference. There was need for treatment and retreatment to curb the infection. But as late as 1948, according to the Government's own Agriculture Department Report of that year, only areas of scattered outbreaks in the Volta Region had been treated, with retreatment already started. In the Eastern Region and Asante outbreaks discovered had been treated. The Western Region outbreaks had not been tackled; so also were areas of mass infection.[49]

The Government's long delay in tackling the disease problem aggravated it. Even when a start was made there was no real commitment. The slow rate of progress was attributed to lack of staff to carry out government rehabilitation policies.[50] The London Cocoa Conference asserted that Government was not pursuing staff recruitment with sufficient energy.[51] The other important reason for failure, namely, the non-co-operation of the cocoa farmers in the cutting out exercise relates to a communication gap between government and people as well as the natural conservative attitude of peasant farmers, untouched by the government's lukewarm pursuit of its own rehabilitation programme. Consequently, peasant resistance to cutting out of diseased trees remained strong throughout the late 1940s and early 1950s.[52]

NOTES

1. The present administrative areas have evolved gradually, bearing different names at different times; but for the sake of clarity we shall use today's official names. Ghana's neighbours will also be mentioned only by their present official names. Traditional states will be referred to as the people call themselves, and in the case of Asante we shall use the term 'Asante' for the people and 'Asante Region' not 'Ashanti Region' for the administrative area.
2. See Myint, H. 1973. *The Economics of the Developing Countries*, London: Hutchinson.
3. Officer Administering the Government to Secretary of State for the Colonies. 19/12/47, ADM. 1/2/295. The dollar gap arose whenever Britain owed trade balance to USA or Canada which she had to settle in dollars.
4. Saving, Governor to Secretary of State for the Colonies. 13 November, 1949, ADM 1/2/313.
5. The dual mandate theory claims that Britain was in Africa to benefit her own trade and industry and at the same time help the indigenous population to advance towards civilization and progress.
6. Dickson, K. B. 1963. *Op. cit.*
7. *Minutes of the Ashanti Farmers Association Limited, 1934–36* (ed. with introduction and notes by Kwame Arhin, 1978).
8. NAICE/N3 Cmd. 5845 1938. *Report of the Commission on the Marketing of West African Cocoa*. London, HMS Office.
9. Hill, Polly 1959. The history of the migration of Ghana cocoa farmers. *Transactions of the Historical Society of Ghana* iv (1): 14–28.
10. Southall, Roger, J. 1975. Polarisation and dependence in the Gold Coast trade 1890–1938. *Transactions of the Historical Society of Ghana* xvi (i): 93–115.
11. Hill, Polly 1959. *Op. cit.*
12. La Anyane, S. 1963. *Op. cit.*, p. 11.
13. The Gold Coast Cocoa Marketing Board 1952. *5th Annual Report for Crop Year 1951/52.*
14. Myint, H. 1973. *Op. cit.*, p. 30. See also *Republic of Ghana: Economic Survey Presented to the National Assembly by the President, October 1964*. Accra: Central Bureau of Statistics.
15. The Gold Coast Cocoa Marketing Board 1948. *First Annual Report and Accounts for the Year ended 30th September, 1948.*
16. NAICE/N3 Cmd 5845 1938. *Op. cit.*
17. Myint, H. 1973. *Op. cit.*, p. 30.
18. Guyer, David 1970. *Ghana and Ivory Coast – The impact of Colonialism in an African Setting* p. 50. New York: New York University.
19. Guyer, David 1970. *Op. cit.*, p. 51.
20. NAICE/N3 Cmd. 5845 1938. *Op. cit.*; Myint, H. 1973. *Op. cit.*, p. 30.

21. Gold Coast Colony 1947. *Report of the Department of Agriculture for the year 1946–47.* Accra: Government Printer.
22. Myint, H. 1973. *Op. cit.,* p. 30.
23. NAICE/N3. Cmd. 5845 1938. *Op. cit.;* Myint, H. 1973. *Op. cit.,* p. 30.
24. ADM 1/2/255. Governor to Secretary of State for the Colonies. G.C. 120/16/40. Encl. in G.C. No. 99 of 9/2/40.
25. *Minutes of Ashanti Farmers Association Limited, 1934–36,* (ed. with introduction and notes by Kwame Arhin, 1978).
26. *Ibid.* The cocoa hold-ups were the refusal of the farmers to sell cocoa to the European firms until producer prices went up.
27. ADM 1/2/268 September-December, 1942, Encl. in G.C. No. 333 of 30/11/42.
28. Gold Coast Colony 1947. *Op. cit.*
29. Southall, Roger J. 1975. *Op. cit.*
30. Gold Coast 1931. *General Report for the period 1st April, 1930 to 31st March, 1931.*
31. Gold Coast Colony 1931. *Report of the Department of Agriculture for the year 1930–31.* Accra: Government Printer.
32. *Annual Report on the Eastern Province of Ashanti for the year 1930–31.* Accra: Government Printer.
33. ADM 1/2/255, Governor to Secretary of State for the Colonies. G.C. No. 5 of January, 1940.
34. Southall, Roger, J. 1975. *Op. cit.*
35. ADM 1/2/286, Governor to Secretary of State for the Colonies. 12, December 1946. ADM 1/2/288, February to April, G.C. No. 32 of 21/2/47.
36. ADM 1/2/291. Saving Governor to Secretary of State for the Colonies. 15/7/43, Saving Officer Administering the Government to Secretary of State for the Colonies. 7/8/47.
37. Rhodie, Sam 1968. The Gold Coast cocoa hold-up of 1930–31. *Transactions of the Historical Society of Ghana* ix: 105–118.
38. Gold Coast Colony 1931. *Op. cit.*
39. *Report on the Eastern Province for the year 1930–31,* Accra: Government Printer.
40. *Annual Report on the Social and Economic Progress of the People of the Gold Coast 1931–32.* Accra: Government Printer.
41. Gold Coast Colony 1955. *Annual Report of the Department of Agriculture for the period 1st April 1954 to 31st March, 1955.* Accra: Government Printer.
42. Gold Coast Colony 1931. *Op. cit.*
43. *Ibid.*
44. Gold Coast Colony 1948. *Report of the Department of Agriculture for the period 1st April, 1947 to 31st March, 1948.* Accra: Government Printer.
45. Gold Coast 1951. *The Development Plan 1951.*
46. Gold Coast Colony 1955. *Op. cit.*

47. *West Africa,* November 19, 1949.
48. *Ibid.*
49. Gold Coast Colony 1948. *Op. cit.*
50. *Ibid.*
51. *West Africa,* November 19, 1944.
52. *Ibid.,* Gold Coast Colony 1948. *Op. cit.*

Chapter 6

THE COCOA ERA: AGRICULTURE

The late 19th century witnessed important changes in agriculture. The release of labour for agricultural work has been discussed in connection with the rise of the cocoa industry. Equally important for the growth of agriculture generally in Ghana was the introduction of prestigeous crops such as cocoa, cotton and coffee. The well-to-do under rural capitalism were attracted to agriculture because of these export crops which linked Ghana with the outside world, and held out hopes for future prosperity.

At the height of the cocoa era, about half the adult male population, a little over 200,000, were engaged in food production. In addition, most rural women were food farmers. By the close of the 19th century, only a handful of the rich farmers were engaged on the cultivation of the prestigeous export crops.[1] But by 1950s, over half a million of the population were involved in the cocoa industry alone,[2] either as farmers, brokers or receiving clerks, etc.

Improved Techniques
The large numbers involved, particularly in food farming, betray an inefficient agricultural practice with very low level of productivity. This was due to the rather primitive methods of farming which persisted into the 20th century. This meant small holdings of shifting cultivation in which farm preparation and seed sowing were done entirely by hand.[3]

In actual fact, an early start towards improved cultivation techniques seemed to have been made with the opening of the Aburi Botanical Gardens in 1890 and a few agricultural stations in the 20th century. However, the emphasis here was on techniques of growing export crops and this was why influential members of the farming population took to export cropping.[4] But even here, there was no improvement beyond the rudimentary techniques demonstrated in the late 19th and early 20th centuries in Aburi and elsewhere. The more enlightened farmers saw the need to improve upon these early techniques. As they could not effect these changes without government help for reasons already detailed out in Chapter 5, they pleaded with the Government on several occasions to take steps to improve farming techniques.[5]

Significantly, Nene Nuer Ologo V of Krobo, the pioneer farming nation of Ghana, between 1939 and 1945, appealed to the Director of Agriculture in the Colonial Government for action to be taken towards improvement of farming techniques.[6] The Ghana press was also very critical, particularly, in 1946, pointing out that "farmers still used the pitifully inadequate hoe and cutlass for ploughing and the Government has never made the slightest effort to encourage people to use more suitable appliances."

These appeals in the 1940s for improvement in cultivation fell on deaf ears. This may be in part due to the collapse of the government agricultural training centre in the 1930s, when because of their inability to become self-employed and the difficulty of finding jobs in the government Agricultural Department, the graduates of the centre abandoned agriculture for other professions. This killed any prospects of improved cultivation techniques.[7] So the only improvement which now appealed to the Government was on the post-harvest products. The peasant farmers were urged to improve preparation of cocoa, coffee, and cotton for export. It was at this post-harvest stage that some mechanization was introduced.[8] Ginneries were set up to gin cotton for export. Some mechanization took place in the preparation of palm oil for export. But no improvement occurred at the cultivation stage until 1948.[9]

As far as the Government was concerned, a strong need for better cultivation of crops arose only after the Second World War. This was because Britain and other European countries were now short of essential items of food and raw materials. In 1948, a number of missions came to Ghana to investigate the possibilities of organizing large-scale production of crops throughout West Africa to alleviate certain world shortages consequent upon the war. Shortage of vegetable oils was acute. So the mechanized production of groundnuts in Ghana and other West African countries was planned. In response to other needs, there were the West African Cotton Mission and the West African Rice Mission. In all these schemes, there was to be large-scale mechanized production of the crops concerned.

In trying to meet Britain's needs in face of world shortages, the Ghana Colonial Government could not just plan improvement of cultivation techniques alone, but, automatically, diversification of Ghana's agriculture as well. These needs influenced the

Government in drawing up the First Ten Year Development Plan. The Agriculture Department was to be organized on territorial basis with the main aim of finding economic methods of cultivation to replace the current hand tillage and promoting new cash crops to diminish the reliance of the country's economy on cocoa. The Department's detailed briefs also reflected these two important assignments, when it was specifically charged to cultivate improved varieties of a number of crops and evolve efficient farm implements for better cultivation of these crops.[10] Apart from the Agriculture Department, other organs were established such as the Agriculture Development Corporation and the Gonja Development Company to implement these ideas of diversification and mechanization of Ghana's agriculture.

Diversification
We now know that what finally moved both the British Imperial Government and the Local Administration to embark on agricultural diversification was the world shortages of certain commodities, which hit Britain and her allies adversely. But other factors also contributed to this development. As already indicated, the inefficient nature of Ghanaian agriculture drew forth comments and pleas for mechanization and, therefore, diversification as well from enlightened members of the Ghanaian public. These pleas, even though they went largely unheeded, should be regarded as one of the pressures on the British Colonial Administration to diversify Ghanaian agriculture. A more important pressure, however, was the ever-present fear of social unrest in the Colony and the Government's desire to avert popular anger by helping to increase local food production for consumption and the standard of living among the people. Even this fear, though increased by war conditions, was not strong enough to actually move the Government to a determined and consistent action. One reason for this was that the British were torn between increasing local food production and promoting food imports from Europe. The war with shipping problems necessitated the former, but as soon as peace returned, the latter was definitely preferable to British imperialist interests. But the pressures for agricultural change continued to pile up. After 1945, war-torn Europe launched economic recovery programmes and, therefore, needed trade with an agriculturally productive West Africa where countries like

Ghana could have their national incomes increased through concentration on agricultural exports and thus create demands for more consumer goods from Europe.[11]

These were the circumstances leading to the launching of the government's diversification programme. Since diversification could not be separated from mechanization, the agencies set up to promote one invariably promoted the other as well.

In 1948, the West African Oil Seeds Mission recommended large-scale mechanized cultivation of groundnuts, millets and maize. To implement this, two pilot schemes, one cited at Amantin in Asante and the other at Damongo in the Northern Region were tried. The Gonja Development Company, i.e. the Damongo Scheme, established in 1949, was a limited liability company charged with carrying out these projects. But everything went wrong. The crops tried gave poor yields; machinery and equipment imported for the project proved unsuitable. The administration was top heavy, the European supervisory staff were not efficient agriculturists. In 1956, the Gonja Development Company was liquidated.[12]

An Agricultural Development Corporation was established after the Second World War as part of the move to produce goods to rectify shortages in war-torn Europe. Such units as Gonja Development Corporation which carried out the specific projects were subsidiaries of the Agricultural Development Corporation which, *inter alia,* was to develop food and export crops on estate lines with heavy machinery.

It is clear that state involvement in agriculture was very slight until 1940s and when large state involvement first occurred it was more to satisfy needs in Europe than in Ghana. In 1920, agriculture had only 1 per cent of the total proposed expenditure. In 1951, it has only 5 per cent.[13] This long neglect resulted in low productivity,[14] in spite of African efforts in some quarters to improve agriculture.[15] The work of the ADC did not rectify the situation.

Agriculture Department and Problems of Agriculture

In the 1950s, the Agriculture Department's role in these development projects was not different from its 1930–31 assignments. These included accelerating the agricultural co-operative movement in order to provide the basis for financing agriculture;

collecting information on crops, technical farming methods; distributing sound information and advice to farmers; experimenting with crops to find an alternative to cocoa and form co-operative societies to promote these crops, and provide plants and seeds to farmers.[16]

Foremost among the crops the Government favoured were bananas.[17] Others were oil palm, coconut and coffee,[18] pineapples, and groundnuts,[19] and as late as 1957, (under the independent Government of Ghana) only castor oil, rice and food stuffs were added to the list.[20]

Some effort was made to implement these programmes, but the Agriculture Department's contribution seemed to centre on seeds distribution. As early as 1918, the Department had already specialized in this kind of activity and yet long afterwards in 1955 it was doing no more than distributing to farmers oil palm, coconut and coffee seedlings.[21]

The hindrances to the government's agricultural development programmes were many. Paradoxically, the Government's own agricultural policies on local food production and agricultural extension services were unclear for decades preventing positive progressive steps being taken in these areas.[22] Uncertain policies bred a lukewarm attitude to agricultural problems. Such examples as the Government ignoring drought or caterpillar attack on millet, a staple food in the Gonja district of the Northern Region,[23] dismissing, as late as 1940, cocoa spraying as too expensive and instead opting for biological control methods for diseased cocoa trees[24] and yet not being able to import the anti-pest insects from overseas, abound. This British official weakness did not augur well for agriculture since a whole lot of crop production projects like importing disease resistant cocoa seedlings and rooted cuttings from Trinidad through Kew Gardens, London, simply foundered on official inertia.[25] In 1943, what the British Administration considered crucial in proposals for irrigation which "may be one of the most important factors in the future development of agriculture in West Africa" was whether or not Mr. C. J. Rae, the irrigation and drainage engineer visiting Ghana from Sierra Leone, was entitled to an honorarium.[26]

Lack of qualified staff in the Department of Agriculture was, to a large extent, an outcome of this official lukewarm approach to agriculture, and the Government's defence in connection with the battle against cocoa diseases, that "owing to the war demands it has not been possible to maintain sufficient staff to conduct surveys and treatment on an adequate scale"[27] cannot be wholly accepted.

This lack of staff involving many vacancies in the establishment for professional and technical personnel in the Agriculture Department was a serious drawback to agricultural development in the country. First, owing to shortage of qualified man-power, research in agriculture was grossly inadequate.[28] The many steps to be taken including experimenting, collecting information about varieties, yields, effects of manuring etc. before a crop could be established in the diversification programme needed highly-qualified personnel, hence its non-availability meant absence of skills and facilities for dealing with any other crop apart from cocoa.[29]

In face of this typical lukewarm approach to Ghana's agricultural problems, the problems grew unmanageable. Half-hearted efforts to correct the wasteful farming methods, among other things, meant neglect of propaganda and serious agricultural extension work among peasant farmers.[30] This caused lack of understanding and non-penetration of the customs and social framework of African communities which accordingly remained a strong barrier to progress, particularly in soil fertility and preservation improvement programmes launched by government as better cultivation techniques.[31]

Perhaps less intransigent than social barriers were diseases and pests but their hindrance to diversification and other agricultural development efforts were no less important. Long neglect of research and proper attention to peasant agriculture resulted, as we know, in the industry being riddled with disease and this affected agricultural development programmes in various ways. In the first place, these programmes were affected financially because of the total vote for agriculture, disease and pest control took the lion's share, leaving little or nothing for mechanization and diversification. In 1954, for example, the Cocoa Marketing Board which had reserves earmarked for cocoa improvement projects paid out a total of £2,250,000 for the cocoa rehabilitation scheme alone.[32] A decade after World War II, the Board spent £16,625,553 on fighting swollen shoot and capsid diseases.[33]

Quite early in the century, the British Colonial Administration expected agricultural co-operatives to fund agriculture but since low producer prices robbed them of capital accumulation they could not fulfil this role.[34] Apart from co-operatives, the Central Government also identified Local Authorities as useful agencies for funding agriculture. This politico-economic structure started functioning when District Councils began funding agricultural production from their own resources towards the end of the colonial period. But with the coming of a new political order this economic practice changed. In an emerging nation centralization dictated large public corporations in place of district councils as agents of agricultural development. But the public corporations were inefficient, dissipating funds earmarked for agricultural improvement.[35] It was because of these financial problems that the allocation of huge funds to disease and pest control hindered positive agricultural development, all the more.

Similarly, the little staff available in the Agriculture Department became preoccupied with cocoa disease and pest control to the exclusion of positive development projects in agriculture. The work involved for such meagre staff was tremendous. To achieve cocoa disease and pest control, for instance, the staff had to survey cocoa-growing areas in the whole country, to ascertain limits of cocoa cultivation, the age and state of the cocoa, the extent of the swollen shoot disease and the incidence of the insect pest *Sahlbergella*.[36] Add to these, other measures to counteract losses from black pod and capsid attack and you see why the Department of Agriculture could hardly find the time and staff for diversification.[37]

Worse still, disease had a direct effect on diversification in that it killed off a large number of crops thus discouraging their continued cultivation by the peasant farmers.[38] So the plan to cultivate these crops as alternatives to cocoa could not work.

For the reasons discussed above, several crops with the potential for development as alternatives to cocoa could not realize that potential. They included coconuts, banana, citrus, groundnuts and cotton. In 1932, the Department of Agriculture, as a result of decreased staff and votes, withdrew from Atwabo Coconut Plantation which the Government had earlier started in Axim area.[39] In the Keta-Ada district, where lay the country's largest coconut plantation at the time, the disease known as Cape St. Paul wilt killed off coconut trees from about 1940 and by 1957 the rate of damage was simply dramatic.[40] Careful survey of the cotton industry revealed in 1949 that the incidence of diseases and pests were too high in Ghana to make conditions conducive for large-scale cotton cultivation. At the same time, citrus in the Central Region and bananas in the Western Region were devastatingly hit by disease. Maize suffered such serious epidemics that in 1950 there was a 50 per cent shortfall in production.[41] It was also noticed that there was potential for growing soya beans and tobacco but these were not being grown on any large scale. Besides, until 1948, no encouragement was given to rice and groundnut production, also with great potential.[42]

Proof of failure of government agricultural development programmes could be discerned in a comparison with German achievements in the Volta Region; then known as Togoland. In the 1940s, the view was strongly held, even by Ghanaian colonial officials that before 1914–1918 war Germany paid attention to agricultural development in the Volta Region so well that "more use was probably made of coffee, cotton, and other tropical product from Togoland than is now made by Britain."[43] Indeed, since the Volta Region came under British mandate after the 1919 Treaty of Versailles, of the rice, tobacco and maize crops grown in the southern section, only maize was of some importance. Agricultural production declined steadily. The palm kernel crop from the Kpandu-Anfoe area dropped by over 50 per cent between 1936 and 1940, and the cotton crop, of which a small exportable surplus was obtained around the Kpandu and Golokwati areas under German rule "has practically disappeared".[44]

But perhaps the most tragic indication of the failure of Government agricultural development programmes in diversification and improved cultivation techniques was the failure of peasant farmers, thanks to lack of propaganda and adequate extension work, to see any value in soil enrichment efforts of government. This resulted in their refusal to use compost offered them by the Agriculture Department. In this way, peasant farmers in the Northern Region failed to increase yields of maize, millet and groundnuts and avoid the perennial outbreaks of famine in such districts as Mamprussi. Worse still, the peasant farmers, having failed to appreciate the value of raising the fertility of the light sandy soils of the north,[45] have unwittingly condemned future generations to poor harvests and perpetual poverty. The problem was so intractable that the Government terminated all efforts for change and openly resigned itself to the situation, only hoping for "an improvement of output within the existing agricultural system".[46]

Failure of Agricultural Co-operatives

We have seen how the attempt to use co-operatives to finance agricultural development failed. The co-operatives were also expected to help in various other ways to improve farming techniques. In particular, local farmers, as members of co-operatives, were to have access to modern machinery and techniques. But with the coming of the Nkrumah regime and its emphasis on centralization, the co-operatives found themselves in a dilema. If they towed the line, most of their energies would go into politics, and if they did not, they would be replaced by the CPP-dominated United Ghana Farmers Council, and this indeed happened in 1961. With the collapse of the co-operatives came the end of more seasoned efforts at agricultural improvement. The United Ghana Farmers Council did not have experienced officers dedicated to the cause of agricultural improvement, such as those gradually emerging under the now neglected co-operative movement.[47] Even though the co-operatives were restored in 1966, they had been deprived of most of their resources and they could not find their feet easily.[48] Agricultural development was the victim of all these changes directed to politics rather than economic growth.

State Farms

The new Ghanaian regime from 1957 was dissatisfied with the traditional agricultural sector,[49] which could not cope with increased food demands of a growing population. It was disenchanted with the Agricultural Development Corporation because of its origin,[50] and non-performance resulting in increased and crippling food and raw material imports. The new Government, therefore, addressed itself to the problem on different lines. In 1960, it dissolved the Agricultural Development Corporation and established the State Farms Corporation in January 1963 to undertake large scale mechanized farming.

The State Farms Corporation had its head office in Accra for overall planning, policy making and administration. Smaller regional headquarters were in charge of specific crops and farms in each region. Each farm had a manager, and technical staff as well as a farm committee which apart from ensuring yearly production targets had to strengthen party activities in the corporation.[51] The corporation took over management of the Ministry of Agriculture's stations and projects started by the defunct Agricultural Development Corporation. It also took over cocoa trial and demonstration stations.[52] It inherited 42 farms in 1963; by 1966 it increased them to 105. On these farms it cultivated 13,796 hectares of permanent crops e.g. oil palm, coconut, kola banana and rubber, and 8,600 hectares of food crops. State Farms Corporation also carried out rearing of fowls, animals and raised sugar plantations. Agriculture during this period, 1959–1965 had increased votes i.e. 8 per cent under 1959 plan and 14 per cent under 1963/1964 plan.[53] But in 1964, large-scale farming including State Farms Corporation represented only 1 per cent of the total cultivated area, and of this State Farms Corporation owned 100,000 hectares. Only 82,000 hectares of the total 405,000 hectares acquired by all large-scale farms were cleared and only 40,000 hectares were put under crops. Of this, State Farms Corporation cropped 50 per cent of the cultivated area, i.e. about 20,000 hectares; the remaining field was cropped by co-operatives, Brigade Farms and other institutional farms.[54] State farms failed to make an impact on the agricultural scene.

Reasons for the failure of the State Farms Corporation included lack of adequate trained personnel at all levels. Particularly, competent field staff was hard to come by. The workers were often disobedient and unruly and this affected the smooth operation of the farms. Managers too were sometimes fraudulent and a number of farms reported to headquarters as operating had never in fact been established. Management was generally so weak that headquarters tried to direct daily activities at the farm level and were therefore forced to take ad hoc decisions without basic information on the conditions of the farms concerned.[55] The farm committee, as indicated, had political duties and these turned out to be covering inefficiency with protestations of loyalty to Nkrumah and the Convention People's Party. The hiring of large numbers of redundant labourers in an effort to reduce nationwide unemployment was also political and meant that the State Farms Corporation could not function economically.[56] Amidst this wastage, large scale mechanized farming, which because of heavy overheads could not normally compete favourably with peasant food farming, proved totally inadequate to the task of food production. The State Farms Corporation tree and industrial crop projects could also not show enough promise before the 1966 coup d'etat terminated yet another effort at large scale and improved farming.

One other state organisation for agriculture started in 1961 as a Builders Brigade, building roads and doing other constructional work; but soon shifted to agriculture as Workers Brigade. The members were paid 6 shillings and 6 pence a day. They established farms all over the country, but there were too much corruption and inefficiency in the Brigade Camps to make the venture worthwhile.

Export Crop Production

Oil palm
It should be clear by now that for Ghana to improve upon its 19th century palm oil production, fruit-picking from wild groves should give way to proper cultivation of palm trees and mechanization should replace traditional methods in oil extraction. It was largely because cultivation problems did not receive adequate attention that Ghana's oil palm industry failed to expand in face of growing scientific oil palm farming elsewhere in the world, particularly in Far Eastern Countries.

Oil palm cultivation met with problems early in the 20th century. The main problem was loss of labour to cocoa cultivation with a higher cash reward. The producer price of palm products began to decline in the 1920s and palm oil in particular was going into domestic consumption and so not much of a cash earner.[57] As such, heavily-capitalized plantations were uneconomical and were, in fact, ruled out by the 1926 West African Oil Palm Industry Conference in Nigeria. Ghana's oil palm industry like that of Nigeria was overtaken by modernized oil palm estates in Malay and Sumatra.[58]

As production declined, there were increasing problems in the extraction process. Post-harvest preparation unlike cultivation received some attention from firms and government officials. A few oil mills were established before 1930. United Africa Company Limited built some of these mills. Palm Oil Estates Managers Limited also built a mill at Sese near Takoradi. As these mills incurred losses owing to insufficient fruit supply for processing, the Government in 1931 introduced a subsidy scheme for mill-owners losing because of insufficient supply of fruits. So Palm Oil Estates Managers Limited built another mill, the Bukunor Palm Oil Mill.[59] In the same year, the United Africa Company Limited also built another mill at Atter-Poponya.

Up to the early 1940s, the low producer price of palm products continued, causing Ghanaians to lose interest in the industry altogether.[60] The situation was so bad that the firms and the Government had a rethinking about the post-harvest mechanization. A hand press with only a little outlay would obviate the losses incurred in the expensive high capacity oil mills. So the United Africa Company Limited, once again, took the initiative and introduced a Duchscher oil press. The Department of Agriculture demonstrated to the farmers the use of this press as well as kernel-cracking machines but no real interest was evoked in the industry, even though in 1948 prices rose in response to worldwide shortage of oils and fats.[61]

The growing demand for vegetable oil after the Second World War brought fresh hopes for reviving the oil palm industry. Mill losses were considered no longer a threat and indeed a large vegetable oil mill to extract not only palm and kernel oil, but also groundnut and coconut oil was now planned.[62] The perenial problem of poor cultivation and harvests was also for the first time seriously tackled. When the Agricultural Development Corporation was formed it established large-scale oil palm plantations. With the liquidation of the Agricultural Development Corporation, the State Farms Corporation took over its oil palm estates. Concentration was on improved seeds and the use of fertilizers for better yields. But these efforts came too late; their impact on the oil palm industry was limited. By 1960, more than half of Ghana's oil palm trees were over 20 years old, with only 10 years of productive life left. In 1965, the State Farms Corporation had 3,500 hectares of trees but 800 hectares were over 30 years of age, and required replanting. Only 1,560 hectares were actually producing.[63] So the Ghana oil palm industry remained in the doldrums.

Rubber

It has been shown that rubber, as an export crop, was another contributor to the 19th century Ghanaian economy. But during the 20th century, Ghana's rubber production experienced ups and downs with the varying fortunes of world trade.[64]

The first quarter of this century saw rubber production in decline but there was a brief revival of rubber exports from 1923. When world trade went into depression, rubber production followed suit except for a few years during World War II. Rubber prices were low, mainly because of the depression in world trade.[65] The shortage of labour on rubber plantations was partly a result of the costliness of that labour, but the chief cause here was the competition with cocoa which drew most of the labour away. By the beginning of the 20th century, European plantation rubber cultivated from imported Brazilian para-rubber, could not reach its 19th century production levels on account of the foregoing conditions. What was left of peasant wild rubber collection was still crudely done, rendering the product very low in quality. Equally disastrous for rubber production was peasant adulteration of the latex to increase quantity.[66] The 1930s thus witnessed very low activity in rubber production.

In 1941, the Government's attitude to this situation was revealed in its decision to assist in the production of rubber only if it was needed to promote the war effort. This was one of the reasons why rubber production lost its vim in the 1930s. An instance of this was that the rubber trees in the Bunsu demonstration farm (near Kibi, Eastern Region) set up through the instrumentality of Achimota College remained untapped since 1935.[67] Such a neglect meant that Ghana's rubber production could not compete favourably with Asian rubber on the world market. Production in Ghana fell from 245,000 kilogrammes valued at £21,986 in 1930 to 100,000 kilogrammes valued at £4,936 in 1931.

It turned out, however, that Ghana's rubber was needed for the war effort, so the Colonial Administration in Ghana initiated the second revival of rubber production. A rubber production campaign was launched in 1941 and in 1942 the output of rubber reached 2,040 tonnes, leading to the highest export of the product in that year since the beginning of the 20th century.[68] But with the return of peace, the need for rubber was no longer pressing and production once again fell drastically.

Ghana under new political direction in the 1950s ventured into industrialization and a number of factories needing rubber as raw material came into existence. Two of these were: Ghana Rubber Products Limited, which produced rubber and canvas footwear, and a Rubber Tire Factory which was opened in 1961 at Bonase. The need for additional rubber supply caused the state to initiate, in 1959, a co-ordinated expansion programme and the State Farms Corporation. From 1960–1964, about 2,769 hectares of rubber were planted. The State Farms Corporation also acquired a new concession of 16,200 hectares and by 1964, 3,736 hectares of new rubber trees were planted and a target was set to plant 15,920 hectares by 1966.[69] But the collapse of the Nkrumah regime in that year adversely affected these new efforts.

Cotton

As we have seen, cotton development was not very successful in Ghana by the early part of this century, in spite of a strong potential for that development. In the Volta Region, before and immediately after the First World War, peasant farmers had shown considerable promise in cotton cultivation, achieving as much as 560 kilogrammes of seed cotton per hectare.[70] Peasant farmers in other areas as discussed in Chapter 4, including the Northern Region also carried cotton cultivation into the 20th century. The agencies capable of providing direction in modern cotton development in the 19th century, i.e. the British Cotton Growing Association and the local British Administration, continued their activities into the 20th century. But between World War I and II, those activities did not go beyond their 19th century predecessors of distributing seeds and ginning the cotton. A third agency was co-operatives designed to fund cotton cultivation.[71]

These agencies concentrated on the Volta Region and Northern Region. In the Volta Region from 1930, experimentation was going on with Ishan cotton to select improved and high yielding strains.[72] In the Northern Region, efforts were directed to getting a type of cotton that would grow best in the light sandy soils. The experiments continued till 1932 when American upland cotton D 28 was introduced in the two areas. However, not much was done between supply of seeds and the harvest. With a number of problems persisting, cotton development in Ghana was seriously hampered.

One of these problems was the poor soil which seriously reduced yields. Low yields also resulted from a variety of agronomic reasons. Insect pests also did considerable damage. Transportation of cotton to the south from the Northern Region also rendered cotton cultivation uneconomical, particularly in view of low prices of cotton in the consuming markets. The total annual production of cotton was about 12,700 kilogrammes. There could be no better summing up of the colonial period of cotton development in Ghana than the warning given, in 1947, to the Empire Cotton Growing Corporation that cotton could not be a major element in local agriculture because it was too much pest-and disease-ridden. Lukewarmness on the part of colonial officials in cotton cultivation was now openly displayed.

It was not until 1957 when Ghana had an independent regime that cotton development entered a new phase, with greater government interest in the establishment of cotton industry. In 1961, the Government's investigations into the potentials of cotton development took it back to peasant efforts earlier in the century revealing a possibility of from 1,630 kilogrammes to about 2,123 per hectare in different parts of Ghana. The State Farms Corporation was given the task of achieving these targets and by 1964, 660 hectares of cotton were established by the Corporation in northern Ghana and in the Volta Region.[73]

Ghana's cotton industry, in the 1960s, was on the face of it extremely successful. In 1961, $60 million worth of textiles were imported into the country. In a few years, this was reduced to $30 million, when Ghana's own textile factories came into production. But the unfortunate fact was that the raw cotton needed in these factories had to be imported. Indeed, it was estimated in 1964 that for 1970 alone no less than $10 million worth of raw cotton, in addition to chemicals, would have to be imported to feed the country's textile mills.[74] Cotton cultivation in Ghana so far did not fulfil the expectations of the farmers. Agencies connected with cotton development left vital matters unattended to for far too long for cotton to rise even to average production levels. The Convention People's Party Government of Nkrumah tackled the problem but it needed more time than it had to rectify the situation.

Coconut

Coconut cultivation, unlike that of cotton, started in earnest only in the 20th century. Before then, however, it would appear that some coastal communities like the Anlos had established small coconut plantations on the seashore, some time after this tree crop was first introduced in the 16th century from the east coast of Africa. A few other coastal communities must have started experimenting with coconuts when the 20th century opened. It was only in the early years of the 20th century that government-sponsored plantations were erected on Christiansborg and La beaches in Accra.

By 1920, the Keta-Ada district, taking advantage of government distribution of seeds, had already established the coconut industry as a leading one in the country. By 1932, some 3,970 hectares of coconut trees were established. Some of the fresh nuts were locally consumed, as was the oil extracted from most of the rest left to dry into copra. Only about a thousand tonnes of copra were exported yearly.[75] From 1940, there was disaster and the trees began to die out due first to the Cape St. Paul Wilt already referred to and secondly, particularly in the Agbozume area, the lowering of the water table following several successive years of drought. The wilt disease became devastating by 1947–1948[76] and it was from the same year that the Agbozume outbreak began.[77]

In the Western Region (principally on the littoral between Axim and Half Assini) peasant coconut plantations were only beginning by 1920 and by 1938 they reached some 800 hectares with approximately 300 hectares more of government plantations. Here, more government interest was demonstrated in the industry to the extent that investigations were not only done, as usual into the post-harvest preparation and storage of copra, but also into yields and effects of manuring during cultivation.[78] Though short-lived, this demonstration of government interest seemed to have strengthened peasant efforts. Between 1937 and 1940, inspite of unattractive copra prices, new plantations were established in the Western Region, particularly west of the Ankobra.[79] An important incentive was that, during and after the Second World War, prices of nuts for local oil production, though not for exported copra, rose, reaching £9 per tonne, and it was the Western Region which was in a position to take advantage of this, and increased considerably its area of coconut plantations. In 1947, the Region took 31,000 of the 55,000 seedlings supplied by the Agriculture Department.[80] Indeed, from 1940 onwards, the development of coconut plantations in the Western Region was said to be successful,[81] at a time that the Keta—Ada district plantations were in decline.

The entire coastline between Ada and Axim was dotted with coconut groves rising at random along the seaboard. The development of the La-Christiansborg plantation was seriously hampered by the outbreak of attack by rhinoceros beetles which destroyed the trees. West of this the next important plantation was in the Central Region, particularly in and around Saltpond, Cape Coast and Komenda and this has grown into a sizeable industry today, ranking next in volume to the Axim-Half Assini and Shama-Takoradi plantations of the Western Region.

Citrus

Quite early in the century, lime cultivation in the Central Region was of great significance. There were hopes of citrus doing well as one of the proposed alternatives to cocoa. The reasons for this optimism included the fact that the soil in the Central Region was suitable for citrus development. Equally important was the fact that, before 1930, Messrs. Rose and Company Limited established a factory at Asebu for processing lime into lime products, and were by 1940 known to be extending these facilities.[82] But the lime plantations remained confined to the Central Region, concentrated in places like Abakrampa and Asebu. Furthermore, even in the Central Region, large areas formerly under citrus began to lose their plantations due to a number of factors. The foremost was the deterioration of mineral status in Ghana's soils generally, these being vital to lime growth; and the lack of water seasonally resulted in some deficiency in the citrus plants and this in turn led to extensive dying of lime trees.[83] Then there was a number of diseases some of which attacked citrus fruits, including oranges and grape fruits,[84] and others which killed the whole plant. As late as 1944 there was no hope of this problem being rigorously tackled apart from a promise of support to the Government from Messrs. Rose and Company Limited, pledging to participate in any experiments geared to solving these problems.[85]

Coffee

Coffee which was also tagged in the late 19th century as a prestigeous crop failed to rival cocoa as an export crop. It now thrives principally in the Volta Region, Kwahu in the Eastern Region and the Asante Region. The Volta Region industry seems to have started earlier than the others, in the late 19th century, under German encouragement and supervision. West of the Volta, the Kwahu Scarp favours coffee and so do parts of Asante. In these places, the main push for fairly prosperous coffee plantations came from the suitable soil, congenial climate and adequate rainfall. The crop has been developed to an average level throughout the first half of this century.

Bananas

In the case of bananas, which had close to ideal conditions for growth in the Western Region, it took little encouragement to develop it. In the 1930s, both individual farmers and co-operative societies took to growing bananas for export. The crop was on the way to becoming an alternative to cocoa but unfortunately the Second World War knocked it off course. From 1941, the war prevented the shipping of bananas as well as certain other commodities to the United Kingdom and the farmers found themselves in a difficult plight, without any other form of livelihood. The Government tried to compensate banana farmers but the rate of payment was so low that this move solved no problems.[86] So declined yet another potential cash crop of Ghana.

Food Crop Production and Livestock Development

Food Crop

Food crop farming in the 20th century has had a great deal of potential. Whenever prices of export crops go down, farmers automatically turn to food farming. The growing of cereals like maize, guinea corn, millet, rice and of tubers such as yams, cocoyams, Hausa potatoes and plantain, as well as vegetables (pepper, onions, shallots, okro and tomatoes) claims the attention of many. But there have always been obstacles in the way of improved food cropping in Ghana.

In the first place, the local Colonial Administration, as

already pointed out, could not formulate a clear policy on food production since on the one hand they supported food imports from Europe and yet on the other they needed cheaper local food supplies to avoid social unrest in the colony. Staff shortages in the Department of Agriculture were not always due to financial reasons but quite often to this lack of drive in this all important area of agriculture. Poor weather and climatic conditions often impeded improved food production. In the savannah areas, rainfall was sometimes scanty, erratic and subnormal. If this occurred continuously for several years, as was the case in the Dagomba district in the early 1940s, food crops failed and famine followed.[87]

Inadequate labour for food crop production, due to attraction by export crops or other sectors of the economy, was also responsible for low yields, as were diseases, parasites and pests especially locusts. Even where the harvest was good the stock could be drastically reduced through poor storage which encouraged weevil infestation in the case of grains and spoilage in the case of vegetables and root crops. Lack of feeder roads or cheap transportation from the farms to consuming centres often contributed to the latter.[88] In 1951, the Department of Agriculture estimated wastages for that year as 12 per cent each for grains and up to 37 per cent each for tubers.[89] There were often resultant serious food shortages in the country. In the Northern Region, this was often aggravated by the farmers hoarding stocks because of poor prospects for the next harvest. In other places like Asante the shortages experienced in the early 1940s were due to transport difficulties. In Asante and Southern Ghana there generally were no actual shortages of food, particularly since there was a number of substitutes on which people could fall i.e. gari and maize for rice, cocoyam and cassava for yams etc.[90] (See Fig 5 on Agricultural Production).

The war years (1939–1945) necessitated a government drive for local food production, since shipping space could not allow food imports and yet the troops in Ghana had to be fed particularly on meat, poultry, fish, vegetables and cooking fat. The restless civilian population also had to be catered for. This was why when the Agricultural Development Corporation was set up, food production became one of its responsibilities.[91]

But if the campaign for local food production had had any vigour, this came to an end with World War II, giving place to the

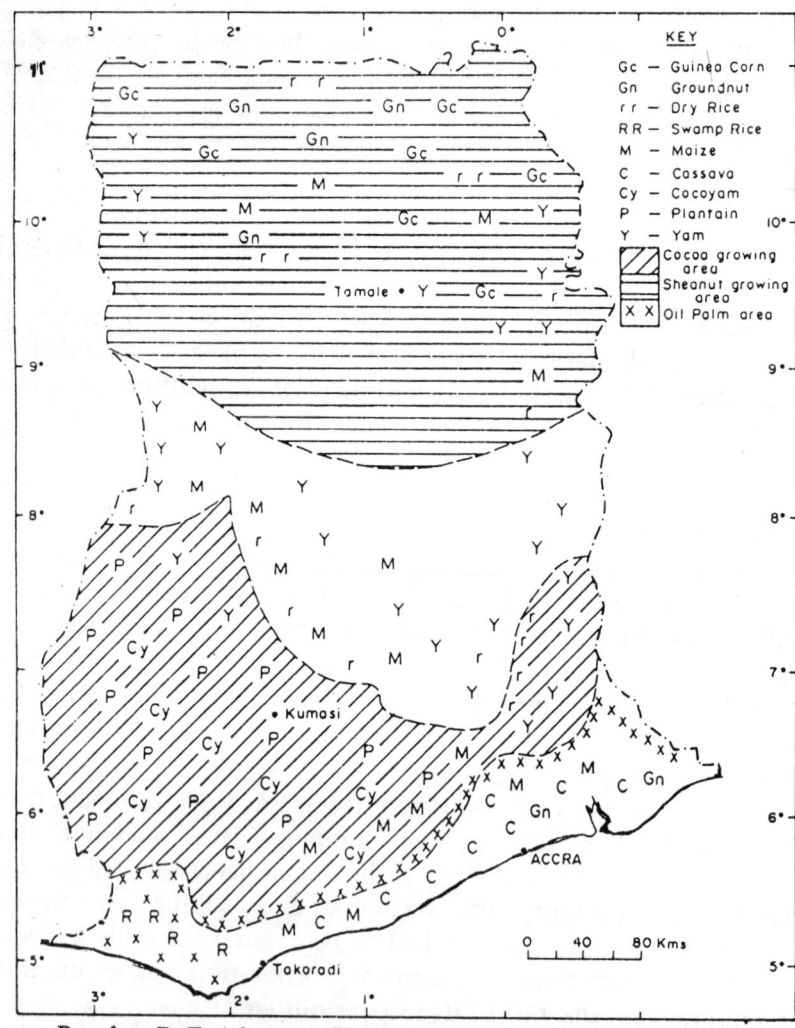

Based on D. T. Adams, *A Ghana Geography*, Fig. 52 p. 104

Fig. 5 Ghana: Agricultural Production

resumption of food imports, which persisted till it changed the structure of demand that could not easily be satisfied within Ghana. Even though there had been increases in food imports before now, such as between 1931 and 1950, when food imports rose from £1 million to £6 million,[92] this cultivation of taste for luxury goods resulted in a much more increased food imports, about 9 per cent in some cases between 1951 and 1961. During that decade, rice imports rose 703 per cent in value terms,[93] and total food imports of which the most important were rice, wheaten flour, sugar, potatoes, fish and meat, rose from £10 million to over £26 million.[94]

Livestock

The livestock situation in the 1920s was that it needed greatly to be improved so as to correct the protein deficiency in the diet of the people. In view of the deficiency, cattle had often to be imported from Bourkina Faso. From 1930 to 1938, the number of cattle in the colony increased from 137,000 to 219,000. This followed the implementation of a scheme of rigorous control of livestock diseases by a new Veterinary Station established in the Northern Region.[95] Yet, meat supply in the country was still inadequate and necessitated increased imports of cattle, sheep and goats over the northern frontier.[96] If this shortage did not awaken the Colonial Administration's interest in livestock improvement, World War II and the need to find dairy products locally for the troops certainly did. There was not just a plan to start a dairy project at the Nungua Farm of the Department of Agriculture but also to extend this project along the entire coastal region,[97] and step up cattle breeding in other areas as well. So it was that in 1942 "mixed farming" experimental stations were established in Lawra-Na and Keta-Ada districts; a station for the development of Yendi Native Administration stock farm for the breeding of cattle that would suit local farming conditions in the north was also established.[98] So by 1945, cattle rearing generally was on the increase.

There were difficulties, however, in reaching the desired targets. Lack of adequate feeding and grazing grounds due to prolonged droughts seriously limited the size of cattle ranches. Secondly, the outbreak of cattle diseases did serious havoc. The foundation herd for the proposed dairy farm was acquired but there was a setback in its establishment due to incidence of rinderpest.[99] With the return of peace and the end of the food production drive, there was not enough will power left for the Government to overcome this obstacle. The dairy project, like other ventures started during the war, was replaced by resumed imports from the United Kingdom. Worse still, by 1945, general livestock breeding was still largely in peasant hands divorced from modern techniques. This was why meat supply was still inadequate.[100] The only exceptions were the Nima Army Pig Farm at Accra and the Pokoase Pig Farm established in 1942.[101]

In 1946, some attention was paid to the problem of establishing general livestock such as sheep, goats, pigs and poultry at centres in Accra and Sekondi. In the same year, the Army Pig Farm at Nima was taken over by the Department of Agriculture.[102] By 1948, Ghana had a total of 300,000 heads of cattle, mainly in the Upper East Region and the Upper West Region, and also in the Accra plains and southern Eweland which boasted of only 5,000.[103] These achievements in cattle and general livestock development could not provide fully for the nation. Thus, imports of dairy produce, meat, poultry and even eggs had to be continued throughout the 1950s and 1960s.

Fishing
Since time immemorial, Ghanaians have developed a fishing industry on the country's rivers, lakes, lagoons and the Atlantic littoral. The art of boat building to produce dug-out canoes for use on the rivers, lakes and coastal lagoons, and later surf boats on the sea was first developed in connection with the ancient occupation of fishing.

During the 19th century, numerous small fishing canoes plied the various water-ways; and river and lagoon fishing became a popular occupation of many peasant communities in the country. Surf boats also go far back into West Coast history but, unlike river canoes, appeared to have been primarily used as a means of transportation in the coast-wise carrying trade between Ghana and the kingdom of Benin in Nigeria. In the 17th century, these surf boats were the major means of communication between the western and central districts of Ghana; and it was only then that sea fishing villages sprang up along the Ghana littoral and the surf boats, based on the pattern of the river craft, but specially adapted for the rough waves of the sea, became invaluable for coastal fishing.

Throughout the 19th century, more and more people on the coast of Ghana took to fishing, while in the interior farming became the predominant activity. The reasons for these developments were mainly geographical; apart from the relatively bountiful supply of fishing facilities provided by the sea, the West African coastal scenery was one of lagoons, creeks, streams etc. which abound in fish supply markedly absent in the interior. The coastal mangrove swamps and the brackish water vegetation of the sea shore was totally unsuited for farming and this compelled whole communities there to take to fishing.

From about mid 19th century to the early part of the 20th century, fishing was highly developed along the major rivers of Ghana, particularly on the Lower Volta. Here, because of facilities for fishing both on the river and in the lagoons on both sides of the Volta estuary, the largest of which was the Keta Lagoon, the people excelled in fishing. Thus, the Anlos surrounding the Keta lagoon and the Adas at the mouth of the Volta river became expert fishermen. The importance of this occupation to them could be seen in the rivalry generated over fishing rights on the Volta, and the effects this rivalry had on political alignments in the Lower Volta basin.

Both Anlos and Adas, but the former in particular, formed companies with well-established hierarchies ranging from the boatswain as the top of the technical personnel down to divers, boat rowers, net menders and other minor ranks. The companies were formed because fishing had often to be done in such distant parts of the West Coast from Anlo as Monrovia, Freetown and even Dakar to the west, and Anecho, Plah or Whydah and Badagri to the east. Every year in August, recruiting agents of the various companies went round Anlo villages offering the programmes of their respective companies to the villagers some of whom joined and were transported to the company of their choice. These contracts lasted a year and the months of June and July saw many of the recruits returning to their Anlo villages in joyous mood. Recruits in a company which failed to make it would, as a rule, stay on in these distant fishing posts till fortune smiled on them. There were also shorter Ghanaian destinations of these companies, notably Senya Bereku, Cape Coast (Ogua) and Shama. These fishing habits went on till, with the coming of independent regimes in West Africa, these Anlo fishermen became security risks in their host countries, and one after the other the companies were expelled and forced to return home to Anlo. Anlo company fishing within Ghana also declined and the fishing villages were transformed into permanent stranger settlements along the Fanti coast.

Other coastal communities apart from the Anlos and Ada which from the 19th century to about 1950 developed fisheries were the Gas in James Town, La and Tema, and Fantis in Winneba and Cape Coast.

Up to 1940, fishing had been well developed. The surf boats for sea fishing were, as already seen, managed by companies or groups and generally small fishing canoes for river and lagoon fishing were also owned and managed by individuals or families.[104] Both types of craft increased in number, reflecting the remarkable achievements of Ghanaians in the fishing industry.

Till now, river canoes or surf boats were dug out crafts made by traditional methods and there were not less than 8,000 of these crafts in use by 1950. By then, 61,200 tonnes of fish were caught every year. The number of people employed in fishing along the Ghana littoral was about 60,000.[105] Types of fish commonly caught in Ghanaian coastal waters included cod, herrings, tuna and salmon.

From about 1944, some significant improvements occurred in the fishing industry. The difference between these new developments and the earlier course of events was the application of modern scientific equipment and techniques, geared to solving problems which had arisen by the 1940s. We have seen earlier that the war caused shortage of essential supplies particularly food; thus the protein needs of Ghana were affected. There were also increasing problems of peasant fishing in the area of transport and preservation.[106] It was realized that the more promising type of fishing was sea fishing as distinct from inland fishing and that it was better for any developments in the industry to be concentrated in this area.

The very first change that the people went in for was the replacement of the traditional surf boats with motorized canoes. This simply involved fixing outboard motors on the traditional canoes.[107] In 1945, an ordinance was passed by the Legislative

Council to provide for the licensing of fishing motor vessels and for the regulation of fishing in Ghanaian waters. These developments were seriously undertaken by the people; and in fact suggestions were made to Government to promote the formation of co-operatives to facilitate the purchase of motorized fishing boats.[108] By 1950s, this aspect of fishing was further mechanized as the Industrial Development Corporation manufactured powered crafts specially designed for local fishermen.[109] These developments were so far achieved through the zeal of the people. The aspect taken over by Government, namely, preservation of fish, especially bumper harvests involved research but it was shelved throughout the 1940s because of the Second World War.[110]

With the return of peace, the main concern of the fishing communities was the improvement and expansion of sea fishing facilities geared to increasing tonnage of fish caught yearly. Some research was done into the preservation of the fish, but it was shortlived. So whenever bumper harvests occurred, there was a great deal of spoilage. Only the traditional modes of preservation persisted and these were not efficient enough for increased tonnage of fish. Efforts at mechanizing preservation resulted in the setting up of a fish cannery factory at Osu in Accra but this was closed down within a few years as poor factory management affected the products which consequently could not compete with imported tinned fish. The establishment of cold storage facilities, however, received a more consistent attention. By 1970s, State Fishing Corporation had cold storage facilities in Tema, Sekondi, Ho, Kumasi, Tamale, Sunyani, Bolga and these could hold 14,500 tonnes of fish at any given time.[111]

In the 1960s, huge sums of money were invested in the fishing industry, but although the Government attached that much importance to it, the industry was not properly managed and the money went down the drain. Between 1960 and 1966, ¢65 million were invested in coastal fisheries by both government and private enterprises. This was to help in rehabilitating fishing vessels, trawlers, and fishing gear belonging to State Fishing Corporation and withdrawing existing ones of undeserving contractors; by part of this rehabilitation work, the State Fishing Corporation bought 12 vessels from the United Kingdom but not one of them proved sea worthy and was either sold at a loss, or abandoned or never delivered at all in spite of full payment.[112] Private companies did better at rehabilitation but they were too few to make any significant impact on the national fish supply.

In spite of the earlier promise within the industry, fishing in Ghana fell short of expectation. In the closing years of the 1970s, the State Fishing Corporation possessed 16 vessels capable of producing about 2,500 tonnes of fish per month, but due to lack of spare parts, poly sacks and paper cartons and fishing rights, the State Fishing Corporation caught only 500 tonnes of fish per month. This was only 16 per cent of the total fish needs of the country. Mankoadze Fisheries and Kaas Fisheries together produced 7 per cent and the off-shore canoe fishermen produced over 65 per cent of all the fish caught in the country.[113] Modernization of the fishing industry failed to make the desired impact.

Forestry-Timber

The West African tropical forests have promoted cocoa, timber, rubber, various nuts, wild life etc. In this section, we shall consider one of these, namely timber.

It was estimated in 1946 that Ghana had between 25,900 and 31,000 square kilometres of Tropical High Forest.[114] The timber resources of this Tropical Rain Forest have been considerable. Log exports constituted the first major activity in connection with the timber industry. It started in the 19th century, and in the early part of this century the increase in log exports proved remarkable. A number of factors contributed to this increase in log export. First, there was, particularly during the Second World War, a growing demand in the United Kingdom for West African hardwoods, mainly mahogany, but increasingly other species as well. Wooden shingles were on order for military use, so were wooden tool-handles. This demand rose from 76,400 cubic metres before the war to about 186,700 cubic metres in 1947. It was estimated that this demand for timber would by 1953 rise to 622,600 cubic metres.[115] Most of the timber needed in the United Kingdom could be found in Ghana. Indeed, about a dozen species were well known in the country. These were advantageously well distributed throughout the forests. Thus, the quantity and quality of Ghana's standing timber supplies were such that the country entered a period of great boom.[116] From a humble beginning, therefore, of between 1,400 and 2,800 cubic metres of logs exported yearly, late in the 19th century, the figure rose to 18,550 in

1938. In the year 1950–1951, 236,000 cubic metres of logs, mainly mahogany, wawa and sapele were exported.[117]

But the timber industry had an even greater potential than log exports. In the first place, an increasing demand in the United Kingdom for lumber or veneers meant that the transportation of wastage involved in log export would be reduced with the export of veneers, milled and cut on the coast.[118] What boosted timber export generally was the Second World War, for which the use of West African hard woods became vital. The manufacture of shingles and tool handles for military use, for example, boosted timber exports.[119] Furthermore, it was because of the war that the local Colonial Administration in Ghana extended sponsorship to the industry. In 1941, the Government was ready to sponsor, financially, a co-operative society and help it in felling trees for timber,[120] so much needed to be exported for United Kingdom's military use. Later in 1950, further government promotion took the form of extensions to Takoradi harbour which provided improved facilities for handling of logs and the handling and storage of sawn timber for export.[121]

However, the greatest advantage enjoyed by the timber industry was the rise of local entrepreneurship in the saw milling industry. A number of local firms prior to the Second World War had engaged in log shipment only, and therefore sawn timber, produced by a few expatriate firms constituted no more than a small fraction of the total timber exports. Until then, the timber industry was largely a foreign concern and represented ultimately a financial drain on the country's economy. Only a small timber export revenue was returned to the local government's coffers. As late as 1950, that revenue was only £90,000, while the value of timber exported reached £4 million.[122] The foreign timber companies' huge profits were of course retained in Europe, leaving behind a raped forest in Ghana. It was when the industry boomed after the rise of marked African participation that the quantities of taxed timber exports began to rise steadily.[123] In this respect, however, it was not government revenue but the profits of African entrepreneurs which were more beneficial to the country's economy. By 1947, the number of large modern saw mills was on the increase.[124] Export of sawn timber was 3,544 cubic metres in 1944; 57,438 cubic metres in 1950, and 84,900 cubic metres in 1960.[125] In 1950, the timber (log and sawn timber) export value of £4 million represented 5 per cent of the total export value of Ghana. In 1960, timber alone accounted for 14 per cent of the national export value.[126] The African share of this rose naturally.

Even though African participation raised hopes of diminishing the exploitative nature of the timber industry, it unfortunately brought with it serious problems when speculators of all kinds became contractors, middlemen and shippers. Many had little interest in the industry and disappeared from the scene as soon as they came up against some difficulties. They did a lot of harm at all levels, sometimes felling trees and leaving the logs to rot in the bush.[127]

Although disease was not wholly the result of this disorderly exploitation of the rain forest, it was to a large extent caused by it. Borer attack and stain of logs were caused by the slow extraction from the forest after felling. The common damages were by a species of beetles which are the principal wood-boring insects in Ghana. Not much was known about the habits of the various wood-boring insects because of lack of adequate research into their activities; hence no proper guidance was available for contractors.[128]

These problems of disorderly log felling and its consequences were in part due to a tradition of poor control when it was mainly an expatriate business and when the number of contractors was small. With the attraction of many more into the business, the rules governing concessions and felling agreements should have been strictly enforced, but they were not. These rules covered the exercise by the Chief Conservator of Forests of his powers of prescribing conditions, restrictions and limitations necessary to ensure the orderly and proper exploitation and management of all forest resources. In the case of timber, he needed at the time of the rush to enforce the rules by refusing registration of new property marks and withdrawing existing ones of undeserving contractors; by inspecting valid Property Mark Certificates and the logs, making sure that poor quality logs were not transported to the coast for export.[129] Above all, the Chief Conservator of Forests should have insisted on replanting of trees by contractors to replace every tree felled to prevent deforestation of the country. His failure to do this did untold harm to the country.

Other problems include transportation, shipping and storage difficulties, lack of equipment and adequate marketing facilities.

Logs are heavy items and it is always an advantage where facilities exist for floating them on rivers, creeks and lagoons to the ports as in Nigeria. An extensive road system in the first half of the 20th century was not enough compensation for Ghana timber export, because they were built as light roads to open up the country to British influence and not specifically for heavy timber traffic, which consequently shortened their life span.[130] The railway from Takoradi to Kumasi provided a much needed service, but the rapid growth of the industry between 1945 and 1950 put a strain on rail transport as well.[131] Timber-conveying wagons were in short supply as indeed were felling equipment.[132]

Takoradi harbour, from where the timber was exported, had no storage facilities, and the habour area came to be used for log storage, causing congestion and confusion. There were also sawn timber storage problems because shipping facilities were not enough to allow quick evacuation of sawn timber. Thus, briefly, shortage of rail capacity, inadequate harbour facilities, shipping delays and shortage of shipping were serious problems which prevented the timber industry in the 1950s and 1960s from becoming a leading export produce in Ghana. From the early 1960s, there was a sharp fall-off in the export of timber. With the establishment in 1960 of the Timber Marketing Board first to handle the sale and export of wawa and later other species, incentive in the industry diminished. The industry never recovered even though later policies left producers free to make their own marketing arrangements.[133]

Two distinguishing features of the Ghana timber industry, therefore, were that in the first place, a number of circumstances has robbed the country of its fair share of the value of timber so far extracted from its forests. Secondly, and far worse, the manner in which the timber was extracted constituted a rape of Ghana's virgin forests and serious threat to the country's major life support system.

NOTES

1. Lawson, Rowena, M. 1957. Ghana in economic transition. *The South African Journal of Economics* 25: 103–114. Gold Coast Colony 1932. *Report of the Department of Agriculture for the Period 1st April, 1931*

to 31st March 1932. Accra: Government Printer.
2. Birmingham, Neustadt, L. and Omaboe, E. N. (ed.) 1966. *Op. cit.*, p. 238.
3. Lawson, Rowena, M. 1957. *Op. cit.*
4. La Anyane, S. 1963. *Op. cit.*, p. 16.
5. Legislative Council Debates Session 1945, March, 1945.
6. Saving Officer Administering the Government to Secretary of State for the Colonies. 18/9/46.
7. Gold Coast Colony 1931. *Op. cit.*
8. Gold Coast Colony 1948. *Op. cit.*
9. *Ibid.*
10. La Anyane, S. 1963. *Op. cit.*, pp. 162–163.
11. Lawson, Rowena, M. 1957. *Op. cit.*
12. La Anyane, S. 1963. *Op. cit.*, pp. 169–171.
13. Greenstreet, Denis, K. 1979. The growth of public enterprise in Ghana. *School of Administration, University of Ghana Working Paper Series* 79: 1–50.
14. Ghana: *Seven Year Development Plan 1963.*
15. ADM 1/2/257, G.C. No. 218 of 16/4/40
16. Gold Coast Colony 1931. *Op. cit.*
17. *Ibid.*
18. Gold Coast Colony 1955. *Op. cit.*
19. La Anyane, S. 1963. *Op. cit.*, pp. 169–170.
20. Parliamentary Debates Session 1957–1958 vol. 6. 23/4/57 – 12/7/1957.
21. Government of the Gold Coast 1919. *Report on Agriculture Department for the Year 1918.* Accra: Gold Coast Press. Gold Coast Colony 1955. *Op. cit.*
22. Gold Coast Colony 1932. *Report of the Department of Agriculture for the Period 1st April 1931 to 31st March 1932.* Accra: Government Printer.
23. ADM 1/2/260. G.C. No. 511 of 18/9/40.
24. ADM 1/2/260. G.C. No. 512 of 18/11/40.
25. ADM 1/2/256. Governor to Secretary of State for the Colonies. February to April 1940. G.C. No. 192 of 3/4/40: ADM 1/2/255. Governor to Secretary of State for the Colonies. January 1940 G.C. No. 100 of 10/2/40: ADM 1/2/271 of 18 June – 7 September 1943, G.C. No. 196 of 13 July, 1943. Kew Gardens joined in the inertia. A letter from the Ghana Administration to the Director of the Royal Botanic Gardens as to whether Kew Gardens could help in the transfer of cocoa seedlings form Trinidad to Ghana appears never to have been answered.
26. ADM 1/2/271. G.C. No. 173 of 26/6/43 and encl.
27. ADM 1/2/271. 18 June, 1943 – 7th September, 1943. G.C. No. 196 of 13th July, 1943.
28. Birmingham, W., Neustadt, L. and Omaboe, E. N. (ed.) 1966. *Op. cit.*, p. 231.
9. Gold Coast Colony 1932. *Op. cit.*

30. ADM 1/2/256. Governor to Secretary of State for the Colonies. February to April, 1940; Encl. 3 in *Ibid.*
31. Gold Coast 1951. *The Development Plan*; Gold Coast Colony 1947. *Op. cit.*
32. Ghana Cocoa Marketing Board 1954. *7th Annual Report for the Crop Year 1953/54.*
33. Ghana Cocoa Marketing Board 1957. *10th Annual Report for the Crop Year 1956/57.*
34. Gold Coast Colony 1932. *Op. cit.*
35. Parliamentary Debates Session 1957–58, Vol. 6 23/4/57 – 12/7/57, 6 June, 1957.
36. *Legislative Council Debates Session 1945.* Issue No. 1, March 6, 1945, Government Printing Department, Accra.
37. The Ghana Cocoa Marketing Board 1954. *7th Annual Report for the Crop Year 1953/4.*
38. Parliamentary Debates Session 1957–58, vol. 6, 23/4/57 – 12/7/57, 7th June, 1957; La Anyane, S. 1963. *Op. cit.*, pp. 162–163.
39. Gold Coast Colony 1932. *Op. cit.*
40. Parliamentary Debates Session 1957–58, vol. 6, 23/4/57, 6th June, 1957.
41. La Anyane, S. 1963. *Op. cit.*, pp. 162–163.
42. Gold Coast Colony 1932. *Op. cit.*
43. ADM 1/2/259, Governor to Secretary of State for the Colonies. August to September. Encl. in G.C. No. 399 of 30/7/40.
44. ADM 1/2/257, Governor to Secretary of State for the Colonies. April 1940. Encl. in G.C. No. 286 of 16/5/40.
45. ADM 1/2/256, Governor to Secretary of State for the Colonies. February to April 1940. Encls. 1 & 2 in G.C. No. 130 of 23 February, 1940.
46. Gold Coast 1951. *The Development Plan.*
47. *Report of the Committee of Enquiry on the Local Purchasing of Cocoa, 1962.*
48. *Annual Report of the Registrar of Co-operative Societies for the Period 1st July, 1967 to 30th June, 1968.*
49. Miracle, Marvin, P. and Seidman, Ann 1968. *State Farms in Ghana*, p. 12. Madison: University of Wisconsin.
50. Governor to Secretary of State for the Colonies. 24/9/48.
51. Miracle, Marvin, P. and Seidman, Ann. 1968. *Op. cit.*, pp. 15–16.
52. *Ibid.*, p. 13.
53. Greenstreet, Denis, K. 1979. *Op. cit.*
54. Miracle, Marvin, P. and Seidman, Ann 1968. *Op. cit.*, p. 13.
55. *Ibid.*, p. 16.
56. *Ibid.*, p. 44.
57. *Ibid.*, p.26.
58. La Anyane, S. 1963. *Op. cit.*, pp. 116–117.
59. Gold Coast Colony 1931. *Op. cit.*

60. ADM 1/2/255. Governor to Secretary of State for the Colonies. January, 1940.
61. Gold Coast Colony 1948. *Op. cit.*
62. Gold Coast 1951. *The Development Plan.*
63. Miracle, Marvin, P. and Seidman, Ann 1968. *Op. cit.*, p. 27.
64. *Ibid.*, p. 21.
65. *Annual Report on the Social and Economic Progress of the People of the Gold Coast, 1931–1932.*
66. Miracle, Marvin, P. and Seidman, Ann. 1969. *Op. cit.*, p. 21.
67. ADM 1/2/263. Tel. Governor of the Gold Coast to Secretary of State for the Colonies. 28/6/41.
68. ADM 1/2/269. Encl. in G.C. No. 78 of 13th March, 1943.
69. Miracle, Marvin, P. and Seidman, Ann 1968. *Op. cit.*, p. 24.
70. *Ibid.*, p. 32.
71. Gold Coast Colony 1931. *Op cit.*
72. *Ibid.*
73. Miracle, Marvin, P. and Seidman, Ann. 1968. *Op. cit.*, p. 33.
74. *Ibid.*, p. 32.
75. Gold Coast Colony 1932. *Op. cit.*
76. Gold Coast Colony 1947 and 1948. *Op. cit.*
77. Gold Coast Colony. *Legislative Council Debates 1946.* Issue No. 1, Session 1947, March 18, 1947.
78. Gold Coast Colony 1931 and 1932. *Op. cit.*
79. La Anyane, S. 1963. *Op. cit.*, p. 127.
80. Gold Coast Colony 1948. *Op. cit.*
81. ADM 1/2/255, Governor to Secretary of State for the Colonies. January 1940, G.C. No. 5 of 5 January, 1940.
82. *Ibid.*
83. Gold Coast Colony 1947. *Op. cit.*
84. Gold Coast Colony 1944. *General Plan for Development in the Gold Coast.* Accra: Government Printing Department.
85. ADM 1/2/275. July to August 1944. Encl. in G.C. No. 223 of 26/7/44.
86. ADM 1/2/264. September to December 1941, G.C. No. 289 of 4/10/41.
87. ADM 1/2/271. 1st. June, 1943 – 7th September, 1943, G.C. No. 218 of 31/7/43.
88. ADM 1/2/269. G.C. No. 31 of 28/1/43; Government of the Gold Coast. 1919. *Op. cit.*
89. Birmingham, W.; Neustadt, L. and Omaboe, E. N. (ed.) 1966. *Op. cit.*, p.227.
90. ADM 1/2/271. 1st June, 1943 –7th September, 1943. G.C. No. 218 of 31/7/43.
91. La Anyane, S. 1963. *Op. cit.*, pp. 146 and 168.
92. Seers, Duddley, and Ross, C. R. 1952. *Report on Financial and Physical Problems of Development in the Gold Coast*, p. 8.
93. Birmingham, W.; Neustadt, L. and Omaboe, E. N. (ed.) 1966. *Op. cit.*, pp. 26 and 228.
94. La Anyane, S. 1963. *Op. cit.*, p. 195.

95. ADM 1/2/256. Governor to Secretary of State for the Colonies. February to April 1940. Encl. in G.C. No. 166 of 15th March, 1940.
96. ADM 1/2/269. G.C. No. 31 pf 28/1/43.
97. ADM 1/2/263. Encl. 2 in G.C. No. 267 of 12/9/41.
98. ADM 1/2/265. January 1949 – March 1942, G.C. No. 21 of 15/1/42; Encl. in G.C. No. 78 of 13th March, 1943.
99. *Legislative Council Debates Session 1945,* Issue No. 1, March 18th, 1945. Accra: Government Printing Department.
100. *Ibid.*
101. ADM 1/2/265. January 1942 – March 1942, G.C. No. 21 of 15/1/42.
102. *Legislative Council Debates Session 1946.* Issue No. 1, March 12, 1946.
103. ADM 1/2/301, Saving Governor of the Gold Coast to Chief Secretary, West African Council. 1/7/48.
104. ADM 1/2/256. Governor to Secretary of State for the Colonies. G.C. 186 of 29th March, 1940.
105. Lawson, Rowena, M. 1957. *Op. cit.*
106. ADM 1/2/273. Encl. 1 in G.C. No. 49 of 16/2/44.
107. *Ibid.*
108. *Legislative Council Debates Session 1945,* Issue No. 2.
109. Lawson, Rowena, M. 1957. *Op. cit.*
110. ADM. 1/2/273. Encl. 1 in G:C. No. 49 of 16/2/44.
111. These cold stores now reduce spoilage at every bumper harvest season.
112. *Legon Observer,* II (i): 6–19 January, 1967.
113. This means that traditional fishing techniques are still dominant in the industry.
114. *West Africa,* December 24, 1949; Lawson, Rowena, M. 1957. *Op. cit.*
115. *West Africa,* April 9th, 1949.
116. *West Africa,* December 24th, 1949.
117. *Report of a Fact-Finding Committee Appointed by Ministry of Commerce, Industry and Mines, 1953.*
118. *West Africa,* December 24th, 1949; Lawson, Rowena, M. 1957. *Op. cit.*
119. *Legislative Council Debates Session 1945,* Issue No. 1, March 6th, 1945.
120. ADM 1/2/263. G.C. No. 233 of 2/8/41.
121. *Report of Fact-Finding Committee Appointed by Ministry of Commerce, Industry and Mines, 1953.*
122. *Ibid.*
123. Niculescu, Margret 1957. *Report on Industrialization in the Gold Coast Today with Special Reference to Rural Areas.* Prepared for International Social Council, Paris.
124. *Legislative Council Debates 1947 Issue.* Session 1947. March 18th, 1947.
125. Gold Coast 1951. *The Development Plan.*
126. Birmingham, W.; Neustadt, L. and Omaboe, E. N. (eds.) 1966. *Op. cit.,* p. 232.
127. *Report of Fact-Finding Committee Appointed by Ministry of Commerce, Industry and Mines, 1953.*

128. *Ibid.*
129. *Ibid.*
130. *West Africa,* December 24th, 1949.
131. *Report of Fact-Finding Committee Appointed by Ministry of Commerce, Industry and Mines. 1953.*
132. *West Africa,* April 9th 1949.
133. Birmingham, W.; Neustadt, L. and Omaboe, E. N. (ed.) 1966. *Op. cit.*, p. 234.

Chapter 7

TOWARDS A NEW ERA: MINING, COMMUNICATIONS, TRADE AND COMMERCE, FINANCE

General
From the middle of the present century, Ghana seems to be moving towards a new era. Previously, the process of change from one era to the other did not come out so distinctly. During the cocoa era, however, events turned out to be more dramatic owing to the politics of self determination and the awareness on the part of the people that they could use science and technology to bring about economic change for the better. The country's aspirations in this respect have not been realized but their pursuit has affected the course of political and economic activities from the 1950s.

Areas of economic activities in Ghana which could have contributed to the coming of a new era — the era of industrialization or mechanized industries — included mining, communications, commerce and finance. The timber industry, particularly saw milling, too, could have helped but from the above discussions it is clear how timber failed to form the basis of mechanized manufacturing industries. Similarly, mining could not bring about this desired change due to a number of difficulties.

Mining
Colonial authorities claimed in the 1930s that mining had played an important role in the economic development of Ghana. By this, they meant that it generated external reserves for Ghana and in addition introduced something of the technology of industrial countries into what was hitherto an entirely agricultural setting.[1] But a report prepared for the International Social Council, Paris, has a more apt description of the industry in Ghana:

> Mining is peculiarly extraneous to the total economy, that it has little effect in generating any other investment or secondary incomes. The capital comes from outside, the capital assets of, and the training and skills acquired in, the enterprise are of little use elsewhere, the product and the profit leave the country, and even the wages are to an appreciable degree accruing to employees whose main purpose is to export them.[2]

What actually happened was that since the mines were foreign private property, the profits realized were all exported to Europe. In 1938, out of a total domestic export worth £11,163,000, minerals alone accounted for £6,298,000 and nearly all this amount was retained in Europe by the companies concerned for the shareholders of the various mines in Ghana and the British Government.[3]

Indeed, the question of Ghana losing its wealth through exploitation was a burning issue, particularly in the 1940s, in that Ghanaians on numerous occasions protested against what they regarded as organized looting of their resources.[4] The *Gold Coast Independent* claimed that in this way £90 million were taken out by 1946 in gold exports alone.[5] If we add the value of the other minerals taken out by these foreign companies, and if we consider the fact that not much technical skill flowed from the mining to other sectors, then we shall realize the extent to which Ghana's mineral resources were depleted with hardly any advantage to the country.

Gold

Gold, as we have seen earlier in this work, was mined in Ghana from time immemorial, and by the 19th century it was being produced mainly through the open pit system which Akan gold diggers had developed in Akyem, the Tarkwa area and elsewhere. As already discussed in Chapter 2, the geological formations which housed gold in Ghana were extensive.[6] Indeed, Ghana had the largest gold resources on the African continent, next to South Africa.

Until 1875 when Western European Companies began mining ventures, it was the African diggers that controlled mining in Ghana. But with the coming of scientific gold mining methods in that year, African diggers with traditional mining techniques were displaced; a gold rush by about 400 European companies, with a total capital of £40 million, began. But soon the boom collapsed, many of the gold mines were closed down and gold production declined until about 1930.[7]

From 1931, the sterling value of gold increased. This coupled with improved facilities in communications and health-care in the mining areas gave a new impetus to gold mining in the country and a fairly large number of dormant mines were re-opened. There was heavy capital expenditure on modernization of equipment and the introduction of more efficient techniques in the gold-mining industry.[8] Gold production increased and in 1940–1 it reached an all time high of 24,967.4 kilogrammes valued at more than £9 million.[9]

Although gold mining brought in some revenue to the Colonial Administration in Ghana, this was not impressive. Before the 1940s, tax on gold exports were low and it was Ghanaian criticism of this[10] which caused the Local Administration to increase tax on gold exports after World War II to 12 shillings and 6 pence in the £.[11] The tax on gold was collected in the United Kingdom for both the United Kingdom and Ghana Governments. The portion retained for Ghana would usually be held in British securities for the country. In 1949, for instance, the total sales of gold and diamonds amounted to £7,415,966. Total expenditure was as follows:

		£
1.	Salaries of 798 Europeans	1,374,000
2.	Salaries of 34,314 Africans	1,602,961
3.	Stores and materials etc.	2,648,428
4.	Payment to United Kingdom Government (Tax, dues etc.)	158,575
5.	Payment to Ghana Government (Tax, due etc.)	870,289
6.	Medical and Sanitary Services	150,556
	Total	6,804,809[12]

From the above, we can deduce the following information:

7. Net profit or dividends to the overseas shareholders of the mining companies were £611,157. Out of a turnover of £7,415,966, sums exported to, or retained in, the United Kingdom were those under items 1, 3, 4 and 7, amounting to £4,792,159, leaving £2,623,606 meant for Ghana. But out of the latter sum, only monies paid as salaries to African

workers or spent on medical and sanitary services benefited the country directly. Out of the tax and other dues paid to the Ghana Government, only approximately £385,000 would reach its coffers, and that for use in paying mines police and other services for the mines. The remainder of the income tax paid to Ghana would be lodged in British securities for the country. In this way, Ghana could never hope to carry out any development projects out of mineral proceeds, except, of course, those that directly benefited the mines. Ghana's gains from the operation of the mines were thus largely confined to the low wages paid to mine labourers.

The operation of the gold mines should have resulted in the development of technical training and skill in the country. But both the government and the mining sector failed to give technical training the attention it deserved. The technical hierarchy in the mines comprised the Mining Engineer followed by Assistant Engineer, the Chief Technician, Senior Technician, Technician, Assistant Technician; all were in the senior staff category, and of course all Europeans. Then came the junior staff category of Technical Assistant, and Technical Apprentice.

But facilities for training people even for junior posts were very scanty. Indeed, the only technical school until Nkrumah's nationalist movement of the 1950s was at Takoradi and even this folded up during the Second World War.[13] The Colonial Government did not only withhold support from technical training, as in the case of Achimota College,[14] but also it actively opposed even private enterprise in this area.[15] In the mines themselves, there was a solid opposition among mining management circles against employing academically-trained Africans who, mine managers alleged, were unwilling to work with their hands. They preferred technical assistants and apprentices who would also accept initial low wages and only rise through the ranks slowly.[16] As late as 1949, the mining companies wanted nothing higher than technical institutes that would train just apprentices.[17]

Indeed, the mining companies adopted a 'cheap labour' policy of mobilizing 'brawn power' and not 'brain power' arguing falsely that there was no need for trying to raise labour productivity through education and training, because, so they said, African labour force could not improve since they could not respond positively to incentives of higher wages.[18] The result of this policy was that the mining companies employed migrant labour from northern Ghana which could not be trained for higher productivity because they only came for a season, and were consequently paid low wages to match their low productivity.[19]

The potential of the gold mining industry in bringing about economic change was further whittled away by a number of factors. The industry declined first because of the Second World War, and then because increasing costs of production narrowed the profit margin in some mines and rendered operation outright uneconomical in others.

During the war, essential stores and materials needed for gold production became scarce and so out of the 33 mining companies existing in 1939 only 8 were kept open, 4 on a "care and maintenance" basis until 1946 and the rest were shut down.[20] Production fell from 24,967.4 kilogrammes in 1940–41 to 15,565 kilogrammes in 1943.[21]

High cost of stores and high wages, following persistent mine worker's action, further reduced profitability in the mines and by 1961 many of the mining companies had left the coast. Uneconomical operations in some mines were aggravated by low grade ores,[22] and these were the ones to be abandoned by their foreign owners causing the newly-formed State Mining Corporation to take them over in 1961. The most lucrative mines remained in foreign hands.[23]

The take-over by the State Mining Corporation simply meant that the Corporation was a holding company for all the shares of the mines concerned. The state was not involved in the technical direction of the mines, which were still managed by expatriate personnel.[24] Low productivity due to shortage of technical staff and lack of qualified and experienced staff in face of rising production costs in the mines were some of the crucial factors in the decline of the industry, already weakened by the disappearance of development capital in the 1960s. In 1981, the senior technical staff in all mines were under 200 as compared with 800 in the early 1940s. Gold production declined steadily throughout the 1960s and 1970s and in the early 1980s was only 11,320 kilogrammes per annum. Nkrumah's nationalist regime had realized that unless the mines were Africanized there would be no gains from the industry for Ghana. The gateway to this gain was the training of African technical staff, and in 1952, the nationalists had pressed for the establishment of the Technical Training Institute, Tarkwa, to train craft apprentices as a first step towards the training of Ghanaian Mining Engineers. The Government had asked the Chamber of Mines to be responsible for this latter training, but all that was achieved was some local training of personnel in a few mines to shift boss level. Thus, there was no direct mining technical training in the 1950s.

It was only in 1961, when the Technical Training Institute was changed into Tarkwa School of Mines that a three-year Diploma Course in Mining Engineering began, and the training programmes of the institution were specifically directed to mining for the first time since its inception. From then on, other programmes tailored to mining skills were introduced: 1963 apprenticeship course for mine mechanics; 1972 apprenticeship course for mine electricians; 1975 mining technician courses. So far the Tarkwa School of Mines produced middle level personnel. In 1976–77, when the Tarkwa School of Mines became University of Science and Technology School of Mines, a degree course in Mining Engineering started. However, only when the impact of the newly-trained staff begins to be felt, and until development capital becomes available in the mines, will the decline in gold production be arrested.

Diamonds

The mining of diamonds in Ghana on an industrial scale started in this century around 1919 in the Birim basin, which is the larger of the two diamond fields in the country. It covers an area of 1.036 square kilometres[25] and includes Atiankama, Subinsa, Supong, Abansa and Esuboni drainages.[26] The other location for diamonds was in the Bonsa basin, 48 kilometres as the crow flies from both Axim and Takoradi in south-western Ghana.[27] The Bonsa complex which embraced Pintotum and Nimasin rivers as well was opened in 1922,[28] but is at present not in operation.

Diamond mining is different from gold mining in that no great depths have been involved. Consequently, it has been easy for Africans using simple technology to engage in diamond mining since the beginning of this century. When European companies started operation, African miners competed with them and by

1950s some 12,000 Africans organized in small groups or singly participated in the industry, mining more diamonds than the total output of the three foreign firms engaged in diamond mining, employing 4,000 Africans and 50 Europeans.[29]

Generally, diamond was rated next to gold as a valuable mineral resource that could contribute immensely to the economic development of Ghana. There were good reasons for this. During the greater part of the 1940s, for instance, diamond came next to gold in the size of mining establishment. There were four companies and they employed more workers, both European and African, than either the two manganese companies or the only one bauxite property in the country. There were two types of diamonds, industrial and gem, consequently making the mineral useful in war or peace; and this phenomenon certainly helped in stabilizing diamond prices on the world market. Diamond production during World War II, unlike gold production, was not hit by fuel and stores shortages. Indeed, manganese, bauxite and diamonds made valuable contribution to the war effort.[30]

In spite of these advantages, a number of circumstances reduced the usefulness of diamonds to Ghana. First, somehow, production of diamond as officially recorded fell behind that of manganese. This must have been due to the fact that more of the diamonds actually won went into private hands rather than to companies and so it would be difficult to keep an accurate record of winnings. Two-thirds of Africans in diamond mining were non-Ghanaians[31] and they smuggled a lot of diamonds out of Ghana to neighbouring countries. The export figures referred to were thus mainly company figures and only a portion of African winnings.

Before World War II, those involved in diamond mining tried to get gems rather than industrial diamonds as the former fetched more on the world market. Consequently, production figures were never high owing to the scarcity of gem. But during the war, concentration was on industrial diamonds for their use in producing urgently-needed war machinery, and in fact the Government placed a ban on mining of gems.[32]

Diamond production increased in 1943. But this increase was shortlived. Just the following year, there was a dramatic decline in diamond production. In 1945, there was a further decrease.[33]

Table 1 showing diamond production and export value (1942–1946) explains this.

TABLE 1

Diamond Production and Export Value
1942–1946

Date	Output Carats	Export Value £
1942	940,488	546,874
1943	1,154,624	577,312
1944	900,770	450,385
1945	862,021	431,000
1946	702,004	349,128

Source: Annual Reports of Chamber of Mines

The reason for this dramatic decline in production was that the war for which industrial diamonds were needed was coming to an end. Demand for industrial diamonds slackened in 1944, with the end of the war in sight. At the same time, however, restrictions placed on gem production were still in force. What was more, even in 1943 when the increase of 214,136 carats, representing mostly industrial diamonds, were recorded, export value was low, because of the lower rates for this type of diamond compared with gem. Thus, the needs of war did not increase proceeds from diamonds as much as expected.

Throughout the 1950s, diamond earnings continued to be lower than those of manganese. This meant that revenue accruing to Ghana from export taxes on diamonds was small. In the 1960s, the Government decided to acquire direct interests in the diamond business. In 1962, the State Mining Corporation took over the Takrowase diamond fields, as the fourth diamond mining company. The first three were private foreign companies grouped under the Consolidated African Selection Trust. In addition, there was the African industry which continued to win lots of diamonds in the 1960s.

Manganese

In Ghana, manganese ore deposits are concentrated at Nsuta near the Tarkwa gold mines, with a few smaller fields scattered around the Western Region and Asante Region. The Nsuta mine was for a long time the Western World's principal producer of high-quality manganese.[34]

Although the Colonial Administration in Ghana knew of the existence of manganese at Nsuta by 1913, it was only when the metal was needed for making war machinery during World War I that the British war time Ministry of Munitions made a request for operations to begin in 1916.[35] The local Government complied and monitored the production of manganese for war purposes. In 1923, the African Manganese Company Limited, a wholly-owned subsidiary of Union Carbide Corporation, was formed to operate the Nsuta mine. Later, the Yakau Manganese Company Limited was also formed to mine manganese deposits near Dixcove in the south-western portion of the country.[36]

Manganese was included in the strategic minerals attracting special attention during the Second World War.[37] This coupled with the fact that Nsuta provided battery grade manganese, so much needed during the war, account for the steady increase in manganese production throughout the 1940s.[38] After the war, manganese production, in the 1950s and later in the 1960s, failed to expand and, like gold, the industry had all the problems of lack of capital and personnel right up to the 1970s.

Bauxite

Of the minerals with great potential for the promotion of industrialization, bauxite had no equal. It was not just as useful as manganese or diamond for the war; but the quality of bauxite ore in losing weight on processing, lacking in the other two minerals, makes it economically suitable for developing an aluminium industry in Ghana.[39]

Ghana has over 200 million tonnes deposits of proven bauxite ore in the Asante Region and Eastern Region. This ore was formed from acid lavas, tuffs and amphibolites.[40] Most of the deposits were located at Chichiwere Tinte Hills near Yenahin, 208 kilometres from Takoradi harbour and 56 kilometres west of Kumasi in Asante. South-west of Yenahin are the second largest deposits of Ghana on the Sefwi Hills. These were located at Awaso, in the

Western Region[41] and there were also the Mpraeso bauxite deposits in Kwahu.[42]

From as early as 1915 the existence of bauxite deposits in Asante and Kwahu has been known to the authorities in Ghana, following survey activities of the Ghana Survey Department.[43] The Western Region deposits in Awaso were also publicized in the information media in the 1920s.[44]

In spite of the Government's early awareness of the existence of bauxite in various locations of the country, the Colonial Administration for a long time made no plans for its development. The British multinational company, British Aluminium Company Limited, acquired bauxite far more cheaply (owing to lower labour costs) in Indonesia than it could ever have hoped to do in Ghana of the 1920s and 1930s.[45] Besides, since bauxite requires a costly smelting down process to produce alumina, the Ghana bauxite development project involved another scheme, the Volta River Project which would make available the vast quantities of electricity needed for smelting the bauxite. The Volta River Project was extremely costly. In these circumstances, Britain neglected developing Ghana bauxite. The British Aluminium Company was registered in April 1910 for operation in Ghana. In 1928, it obtained concessions for mining bauxite in Awaso area in the Western Region, but it was not until 1940 that war, for which it was needed but which cut off Indonesian supplies to the United Kingdom, compelled the United Kingdom Government and the Colonial Administration in Ghana to develop the Ghanaian deposits. The British Aluminium Company Limited started operation on the Kanaiyerebo Hill cap near Awaso, acting as an agent of the Ministry of Aircraft Production, United Kingdom. After the immediate needs of war were satisfied, the company continued to produce bauxite at Awaso for its own raw material needs.[46]

Since the bauxite ore was exported to the United Kingdom for smelting, the infrastructural work needed for opening the mine excluded the Volta River Project. Even so the infrastructure was costly, an access road had to be built in the Awaso area. A wagon tippler and Ropeway had to be installed in 1944. The installation of a diesel engine-driven power-generating plant took sometime to accomplish, as did the construction of social facilities like staff housing, stores, dispensary and office accommodation.[47] In the circumstances, very little bauxite ore was produced throughout the war years, as could be seen in Table 2.

TABLE 2

Comparative Figures of Mineral Production during the War 1939–1945

Mineral	Output	Value £
Gold bullion (kilogrammes)	4,123,998	18,612,867
Diamonds (carats)	6,058,683	3,365,706
Manganese ore (tonnes)	2,837,590	7,114,599
Bauxite (tonnes)	317,834	998,110

Source: Annual Reports of the Mines Department.

Apart from its paucity, the bauxite ore was poor in quality, because in its rush to get the mineral, the British Aluminium Company Limited did not have much time to perfect its methods of extracting the ore from the rock. It was only in 1949 that the company introduced a new method whereby more careful selection was practised. On the conveyer belts a more careful manual picking of iron-stone was insisted upon. A pilot washing plant was also installed for freeing bauxite from adherent silica.[48] These improved methods came too late for the greater part of the 1940s and the price of Ghana bauxite during that period was very low due to poor quality. (See Table 2).

By late 1940s, the world price of bauxite went up along with those of other minerals. But Ghana's bauxite mines remained in a poor shape and could not take advantage of this favourable market. (See Table 3). Furthermore, the United Kingdom returned to its traditional Indonesian source of supply after the Korean War. There were no incentives for further improvements in the bauxite mines. Bauxite output in Ghana remained small throughout the 1950s.

In the early 1960s, when the Volta River Project was being executed, Ghana missed the opportunity of developing its bauxite due to the insistence of Volta Aluminium Company on feeding its aluminium smelter, a vital part of the Volta River Project, with bauxite from outside Ghana as a condition of making funds available for the Project. Ghana had no alternative but to accept the situation of her vast bauxite deposits remaining dormant.[49]

TABLE 3

Comparative Figures for 1947–1948, 1948–1949 Mineral Production and Value

Mineral	1947–1948 Output	1948–1949 Output	1947–1948 Value (£)	1948–1949 Value (£)
Gold (kilogrammes)	15,728	19,461	4,786,627	5,922,592
Diamond (carats)	765,399	765,399	4,823,008	1,152,010
Manganese (tonnes)	596,828	670,168	2,301,250	3,006,758
Bauxite (tonnes)	92,520	147,470	262,662	274,701

Source: Annual Reports of the Mines Department.

Communications

As we have seen in Chapter 4, transportation was poor in Ghana up to the 19th century. By 1890, the only roads worth the name were military and missionary roads and these covered only a few hundred kilometres altogether. The rest of the country was served by traditional trade paths with several locations totally inaccessible. The best that the local British Administration did then was to get the people to keep these existing pathways clear of bush, but this was not even on a regular basis. There was no system of roads to boost commerce and favour industrial growth. It was in 1890 that the British decided to tackle the problem of roads more systematically. Even though from 1890 to the First World War, most of the roads built were not suitable for motor vehicles, the position was much better than before. In 1890, the Governor Sir W. B. Griffith appointed an Inspector of Trade Roads. At the same time, he initiated road building. In the first place, the local British Administration experienced a major difficulty, that of lack of labour. To solve this problem, the Administration established the Roads Ordinance of 1894 to get the chiefs to provide hired labour for the road building projects. This was not effective enough and a Compulsory Labour Ordinance was passed by the Legislative Council in 1895, empowering the chiefs to compel their peoples to work on the roads.[50]

From 1901, roads began to be built for motor cars and traction engines. Between 1902 and 1914, a number of such roads was completed. They included Accra-Kibi opened in 1905. Winneba to Swedru, 1908, and three roads built before 1911 in the Keta-Ada districts to facilitate easy communication between the hinterland and the coastal areas. By 1914, the majority of roads built in southern Ghana was, however, bush roads not suitable for vehicular traffic. There were over 3,200 kilometres of such roads by 1911. During the same period 368 kilometres of earth-surfaced roads were built in Asante. Road network in southern Ghana and Asante by 1906 is shown in Fig. 6. From 1903, motor vehicles were introduced into the country but used only by a few merchants until after the First World War, when vehicular traffic became more common.[51]

From 1914 onwards, Ghana reached the stage of building lorry roads and this was done in different parts of the country. There were trunk or major roads and there were feeder roads, and the quality of these roads as well as the distance covered was enough for agricultural produce evacuation during the 1930s. Three different authorities were involved in road-building throughout the first half of the twentieth century. They were the Central Government, Native Authorities and self-help or communal groups.

In southern Ghana, major roads were built in every region. In the Volta Region, the incentive for road construction grew out of the political situation. In 1919, with the expulsion of Germany from Africa, its former territory of Togoland was partitioned between France and Britain. The excellent roads built by the Germans as well as their Lome-Atakpame railway now served the Republic of Togo inducing agricultural produce in the Volta Region, which had no direct communication with the rest of Ghana, to seek its outlet to the ports of the Republic of Togo rather than Ghana. To reverse this trend, therefore, the Central Government in Ghana had to build two roads, one from Adidome

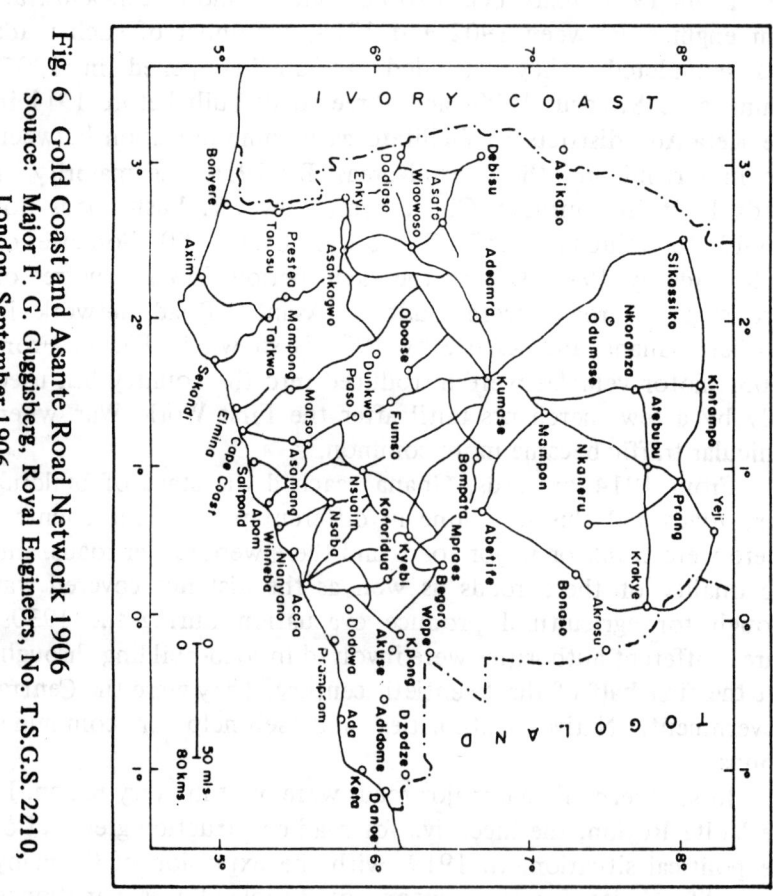

Fig. 6 Gold Coast and Asante Road Network 1906
Source: Major F. G. Guggisberg, Royal Engineers, No. T.S.G.S. 2210, London, September 1906

to Ho and the other from Senchi on the Volta also to Ho. Apart from these connections with Ghana, the Government built more roads in the Volta Region itself to facilitate the movement of goods in the territory towards Ghana. The road from Kpeve to Hohoe reached Jasikan in 1928 and from there to Worawora soon afterwards. Altogether the Government and other agents built 642 kilometres of road in the Volta Region by 1936.[53] Equally important was the fact that the Central Government, in spite of its tendency to shift the burden of road building on to Native Authorities, had to continue maintaining all the roads it had built in the Volta Region. This was because of a strong anti-British propaganda there during the Second World War. As part of the war effort, therefore, the British Political Administration had to prove that its economic activities in the Volta Region were not as half-hearted as pro-German propaganda would have people believe. So it could not leave the trunk roads in the care of Native Authorities throughout the 1940s.[54]

In the Eastern Region, the period from 1914 to 1936 saw existing minor roads converted into first-class roads suitable for light motor traffic. In the Central Region, roads from the sea ports of Elmina, Cape Coast and Saltpond into the Fante hinterland through Foso and Manso to Kumasi in Asante were similarly transformed. It was from 1941 that a number of trunk roads were completed in the Western Region. These included Tarkwa-Bogoso Road and the Obuasi-Brofoyedru Road. At the same time, work on Bibiani-Adiembra Road as well as linkage of this with Kumasi was in progress,[55] and was completed by 1944.

An appreciable distance of feeder roads was also built in Ghana between the two World Wars. These roads were meant to render the agricultural-producing areas accessible to the trunk roads and hence to the marketing centres in Ghana or to the sea ports for export. A few feeder roads were built by Native Authorities, but most of these roads were built through communal labour organized by the people themselves to open up their localities to the rest of the country.[56] Such roads were built mainly in the cocoa-growing areas of the country where there was the need to evacuate cocoa seasonally.

Building roads was one thing and maintaining them another, and the Central Government in Ghana between the World Wars wearied of the latter. Most of the roads it built were passed on to

Native Authorities to maintain. As indicated above, it was only in the Volta Region that the Central Government was compelled by the political situation to maintain 370 kilometres of roads leaving 262 kilometres to be maintained by the Native Authorities.[57]

There were defects in this road system. It was probably adequate for the level of the country's agricultural development up to World War II. But development should have continued to fill in gaps reportedly left in the road system.[58] But during the war, road building was out of the question, except of course the urgently-needed Western Region road system for strategic mineral exploitation for the war. In the rest of the country, all that happened was planning of roads such as the north bound roads and the coastal links that served agricultural areas, but no construction work was initiated for these.[59] An important gap in Ghana's road system then was between Gambaga and Bawku in the Northern Region. In the rainy season, the road from Bawku to Bolgatanga became impassable, so this too needed improvement.[60] But nothing was done about these links until Nkrumah's nationalist Government tackled them in 1956. Still, enough was done between the two World Wars to promote road transportation. This could be gleaned from the number of private cars and taxis imported into the country by the end of the period.

TABLE 4

Private Cars and Taxis Imported into Ghana by 31st December, 1939

New private cars and taxis registered in 1939	327
Total private cars and taxis in use by 31st December, 1939	2,076
New commercial vehicles registered during 1939	778
Total commercial vehicles in use at 31st December, 1939.	5,501

The breakdown shows particularly Ford, Morris and Chevrolet cars and lorries from Britain, USA and Canada.[61]

Plans to develop the mines had led to an early completion of Sekondi-Kumasi railway in 1903. This line had to be reconstructed in 1922. By 1923, the Government completed Accra-Kumasi line and by that date 800 kilometres of railway had been completed. This excluded the Central Region railway linking Accra-Kumasi and Sekondi-Kumasi lines through Akyem, and this was opened in 1927 though its completion over the whole distance was later. (See Fig. 7). Improving Sekondi's accessibility to the interior had to go with improving export facilities for minerals and agricultural produce. So a deep water harbour at Takoradi, which together with the Sekondi-Kumasi line reconstruction cost £4 million, was undertaken.[62]

By 1905, a number of post offices and telegraph stations were established in Accra, Kpong, Cape Coast, Prasu, Kumasi, Sekondi, Dunkwa, Tarkwa and Axim. In 1920, plans for more post offices were included in Guggisberg's *10 Year Development Plan*. The next time these services were reviewed was in 1944 when, for security reasons, telephone and telegraph services were planned for the Volta Region and this in turn prompted the further modernization and extension of existing services throughout Ghana. It was probably also due to security reasons that the Colonial Administration planned in 1944 to establish local air services to facilitate movements of administrative and technical officers responsible for development projects initiated during and because of the war.[63] Effective internal air service however came only with the establishment in 1947 of the West African Airways Corporation, serving the four British West African territories. It provided internal air services within Ghana as well as links with the other territories.[64]

In spite of the foregoing developments, it was found in the early 1950s that communications, among other basic services, still needed extension before industrialization could go ahead. So the nationalist Government of Nkrumah and the Convention People's Party set to work to improve roads, bridges, ports and railways in preparation for launching industrial projects. By 1957 over 1600 kilometres of excellent road were built in the country. The completion of the Volta Bridge at Adomi has greatly improved the communications between Accra and the Volta Region. A new Achiasi-Kotoku railway was constructed and two other short lines were built to enhance the Tema harbour project. Existing lines were also improved.[65]

The post-war boom in trade revealed the inadequacy of Takoradi harbour particularly in handling log exports. Five new shallow-water wharves were constructed to increase port capacity there. In 1954, work began on a new deep water harbour at Tema.

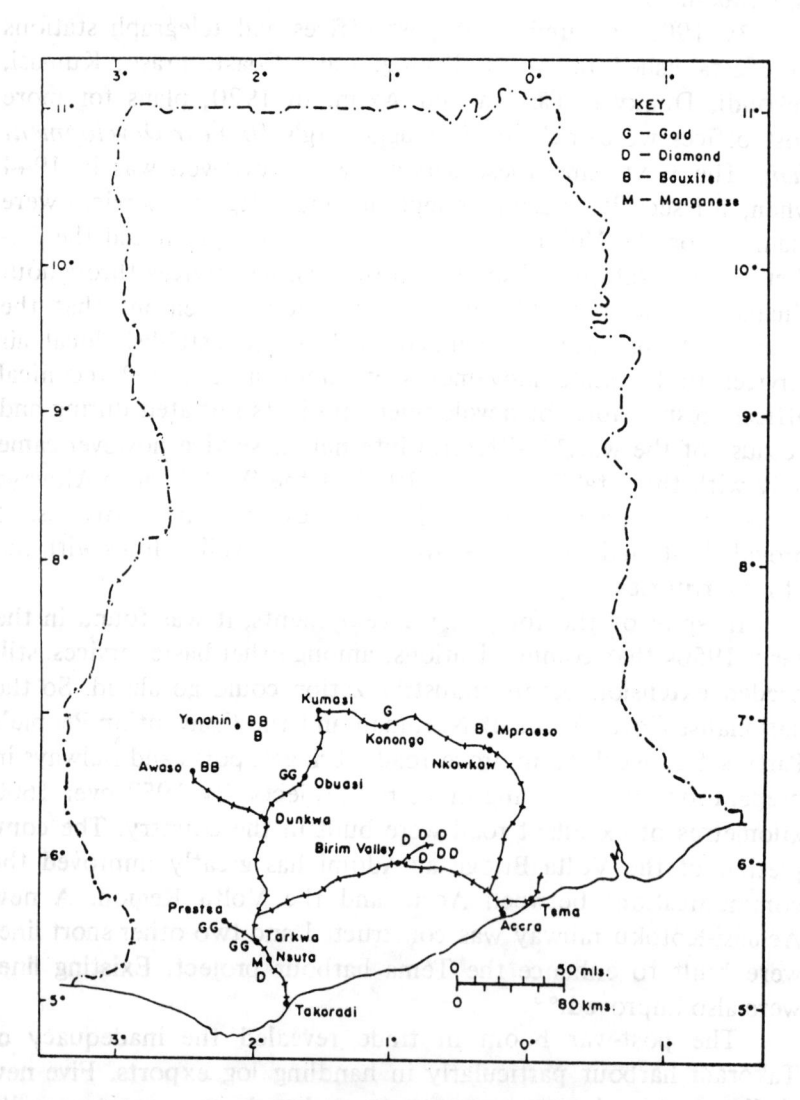

Fig. 7 Ghana: Mineral Production and Railways

Air services were also improved by the training of local air traffic personnel.[66] So the 1950s witnessed considerable advance in communications. But these deteriorated too rapidly in the ensuing decades.

Trade and Commerce
For all countries, developed or developing, trade is, of course, important. After national resources have been developed, the wealth that a country yields becomes available for use only through trade and commerce. Individual farmers, manufacturers etc. receive the rewards of their labours only after trading their goods to others. This reward is normally in the form of money and the more individuals accumulate this the more they store up development capital which they or the state can use to generate more economic activity in the private or public sector. The state further receives direct revenue from taxes levied on trade. Ghana, more than most developing countries, needs trade and commerce desperately, because its mono-crop economy can only survive on the flow of goods and services in and out of the country. Ghana exports raw materials and imports manufactured goods. From the beginning of this century, Ghana's main domestic exports have been cocoa and gold. The principal consumer of Ghana's cocoa has been the United Kingdom. In 1939, just before World War II, total cocoa exports were 286,323 tonnes valued at £5,107,219. The gold exported was 22,444 kilogrammes valued at £6,177,725. Other exports were timber, rubber, lime products, palm kernels, palm oil, copra, kola nuts and bananas.[67]

Throughout this period, there were periods of boom and decrease in trade. In 1936–1937 for instance, even "luxury" items, including pianos, European-made-clothing, malt, liquors and beer were in demand,[68] and when decline came in 1939 it was these luxury items that were dropped from the imports. Cotton goods, mainly Manchester cloth, were among the most important imports.[69] Other items were kerosine, matches, cigarettes, beads and enamel ware. In 1961, exports of goods and non-factor services made up almost 29 per cent of the GDP.[70] Table 5 explains the export situation in the period from 1951 to 1962.

The people involved in this trade were European companies and their agents who, in the case of cocoa, bought the produce

TABLE 5

Value of Exports of Selected Domestic Goods, 1951–1962 As Percentage of Total Exports

	1951	'52	'53	'54	'55	'56	'57	'58	'59	'60	'61	'62
1. Cocoa Beans	68	62	63	75	68	59	56	60	61	59	61	60
2. Timber (Logs and sawn	5	5	9	6	8	11	11	11	12	14	13	11
3. Manganese	8	10	10	5	5	8	10	8	6	6	5	5
4. Diamonds	6	6	4	4	6	9	10	8	8	9	6	7
5. Gold	9	11	11	9	9	9	11	10	10	10	10	10

from the farmers in the interior and brought them to the companies' posts on the coast. Sometimes, Ghanaian brokers provided similar services independently and sold the goods they acquired from the farmers to the European companies for export. With regard to timber and minerals, it was European companies that extracted them at source and conveyed them to the coast for export. In the case of imports, we have seen earlier that distribution of goods imported by the expatriate companies was done by their African agents who travelled up country into the towns and villages with the items. In the 20th century up to 1970 and in most parts of Ghana, the retail trade was almost entirely in the hands of Yorubas from Nigeria, bicycling with enormous loads to the nooks and corners of the country.[72] During Busia's Progress Party Government (1969–72), a lot of Nigerians, affected by an aliens' quit order, were expelled and this disorganized the distributive trade. Another group of foreign traders resident in Ghana were Greeks, Lebanese, Syrians, and Indians, who owned medium-sized shops stocked with goods they imported from different parts of the world.

It was from trade that much of the country's revenue was derived. In 1939, the estimated revenue in Ghana was £4,746,053.[73] The gross Customs and Excise receipts for that year was £2,559,331.[74] So more than half Ghana's revenue for that year came from taxes on trade alone.

What government accumulated through taxes was often for recurrent expenditure only. To carry out certain major development projects, the total savings of the country had to be harnessed. To achieve savings there must be commercial benefits to individuals and the nation. But these benefits have dwindled over the years. Before World War II, there was a pools system used by the expatriate export-import companies to push down producer prices, especially of cocoa. Yet, these same companies imported goods manufactured in Europe out of the raw materials and sold them to the people at exorbitant prices.[75]

Food imports were unnecessarily excessive because the policy of the Government and the companies drove farmers from food to cash cropping, thus necessitating high food imports and consequently losing the country so much in foreign reserves.[76] These multinational companies were extremely powerful and since their aim was to continue their hold on global trade, they could subvert the economy of a country that stood in their way.[77]

Another unfavourable phenomenon was unstable prices of agricultural produce on the world market. Cocoa prices in particular fluctuated widely on the world market. The reasons for this instability were various. The concentration of cocoa production in a single region of the world, i.e. West Africa — Ghana, Nigeria and Côte d'Ivoire — and of its sale in Western Europe and North America could not promote a stable world price of the crop. Because of similarity of climate, any crop failures or bumper harvests due to climate affect the three major producing countries. So it was difficult to control world supply. In the same way whenever the West, i.e. Western Europe and North America, would not purchase cocoa the world demand collapsed;[78] and prices were accordingly depressed. Prices of precious metals, gold and diamonds, also fluctuated on the world market. Whenever the value of the dollar falls people rush to buy gold as a means of preserving the value of their money. The price of gold then goes up. When the value of the dollar rises and no need arises to preserve money in form of gold then the value of gold goes down once again. The process goes on indefinitely.

There came a gradual decline in trade and commerce as the world moved into a recession in the 1970s and 1980s, and European countries set up protectionism to keep out imports of Third World agricultural produce in protection of their own. This affected Ghana already suffering from unstable gold and diamond prices since the 1960s. The effects of unstable world prices for a developing country like Ghana are serious. This instability now and again resulted in unfavourable balance of trade for the country which ran into trade deficits from 1956 onwards.[79] These widely fluctuating export earnings imposed the necessity for the locking-up of resources in large foreign reserves and hence imports of capital goods for development proved unreliable. Even planning for development became difficult, as no one could reliably estimate expected revenue for any year.[80] So generally the ultimate result of fluctuations on the world market was to deprive government of development capital and depress development efforts.

Government's efforts to correct this was to try and get more out of taxes and limit expenditure through import restrictions. It was partly this development that led to government imposing a higher tax on gold exports in 1946. In 1961, this process was carried further. Purchase taxes ranging up to 66 per cent were introduced on a large number of consumer durable goods and tariffs were increased over a wide range of commodities to raise government revenues. Yet, trade deficits continued, and so import and exchange controls were instituted. Import restrictions involved the abolition of the open general licence and its replacement with specific licences.[81]

The harm done before World War II by the pools system was mitigated by the establishment of government-controlled buying agents and later by the Cocoa Marketing Board in 1947 and the Agricultural Produce Marketing Boards in 1949. These boards tended, through their policies, to exert a moderating influence on the effects of world price fluctuations. They stored up reserves so as to cushion producer prices in the years of low world prices, and to lend government development capital in such years. In the 1960s, Timber Marketing Board, Food Marketing Board and Diamond Marketing Board were established for similar functions.[82] But these efforts failed to yield the desired results.

Finance
Under Guggisberg there was expansion in government business. The Audit Department rose to the occasion and gave advice to government departments about the importance of cost accounting and keeping their administrative procedures under constant review with an eye on economy of method. Financial control was quite effective until 1950s when government expenditure again increased. The problems of co-ordinating and controlling the flow of public funds increased. There was insufficient data for policy makers and financial control in the bureaucracy weakened. Careful planning and use of government resources as in the 1940s ceased to influence the nationalist government's financial decisions. The management of the country's finances became chaotic as Nkrumah, irritated by the defective financial measures, would no longer take advice normally given by the Audit Department.[83]

In the circumstances, there were no strong measures to check high prices following salary increases,[84] which could not be avoided under the new political regime. No creative financial arrangements issued forth from the Audit Department and other government departments to serve as investment incentives to the rich Ghanaian cocoa farmer or the wealthy urban elite. So such Ghanaians continued as spendthrifts unable to resist spending the greater part of their income on expensive weddings, funerals and litigation. When in good years income levels were high for the rest of the populace, there were no opportunities for them to save part of their earnings. Furthermore, during the 1950s, Ghana's monetary system was operated under the "Sterling Exchange Standard". and this did not adapt easily to internal development even though it assisted the export sector.[85]

In the 1960s, the catastrophic fall of cocoa prices, particularly in 1964/65 aggravated the balance of payment problems. Balance of payment deficits caused serious depletion of Ghana's foreign exchange reserves. This in turn caused a series of budgetary deficits to be financed by inflationary methods, all leading to a total financial collapse of Ghana.[86]

From 1959, Ghana began to draw on her foreign exchange reserves. In 1961, the country drew ₵ 180 million. So foreign exchange fell from ₵ 356.6 million at the end of 1960 to ₵ 176.6

million at the end of 1961. At the close of 1964, the country's foreign exchange reserves stood at ₵100.5 million; ₵63.1 million of this covered currency in domestic circulation, so only ₵37.4 million was what Ghana had in reserve against balance of payments deficits.[87] In 1965, foreign exchange reserves fell to a mere N₵ 0.9 million and in February 1966 they registered a negative figure.[88]

Two economic features which permanently developed out of this financial impasse were inflation and black marketing. A third result was political instability.

Inflation had been part of the Ghanaian economy quite early in this century, but it was in the 1940s that it became bad enough to attract public notice. The difficulties of the 1940s in Ghana had caused considerable agitation for improved living conditions and increase in wages. A Commission of Enquiry was set up and as a result both government and commercial firms made increases in wages to their employees in 1947. Thus, in that year the minimum wage of Ghanaian workers was some 100—150 per cent higher than in 1939.[89] Farmers also received more money. In September 1948, the Cocoa Marketing Board raised the price of cocoa to the farmer from 39 shillings to 65 shillings per load of 30 kilogrammes. In that year, purchasing power in the hands of the public rose by about £12 million. In September, 1950, the price paid to the farmer for that year's crop was again raised to 70 shillings a load.[90] These developments led to a rise in the price of consumer goods in the retail trade.[91] Even local food prices rose sharply.[92]

Price rise had several causes. It was not just more money in the hands of consumers but also the absence of gainful economic outlets for the increased income. In the 1950s, increased government spending compounded the problem as it did not lead to increased productivity. Low productivity meant decline in domestic supply; so prices further rose sharply. A process like this sometimes corrects itself if government projects, like those of the 1950s and 1960s, begin to yield dividends and take care of domestic supplies after a reasonable period of time. But the very nature of the industries set up prevented this happening and inflation continued.[93] In the same way, black marketing, which began around 1946 specifically because of the difficulty of getting cotton piece goods, whose imports were disrupted by the war, continued and spread to other items in high demand.[94]

These economic woes naturally gave rise to social and political unrest and consequently there was a great deal of political instability in Ghana, starting from 1966.

These inflationary trends did not go unheeded. Until the 1960s, it was the people who struggled in various ways to get the problem solved. As early as 1946, the Ghanaian daily papers claimed that the country earned a lot of dollars through trade and that this money was being used on other colonies. They expected it to be used in improving Ghana's economic infrastructure and increasing the country's productivity so as to limit inflation.[95] The rank and file were also involved in various anti-inflation campaigns. The campaign led by Nii Kwabena Bonne III, Osu Alata Mantse, went as far as organizing a "complete boycott of imported goods".[96] These efforts yielded no permanent results.

In the 1960s, it was this same problem of inflation that was partly responsible for the establishment of a number of financial institutions to provide facilities for local savings in times of increased incomes, and credit to industries to help them achieve higher productivity. The Ghana Commercial Bank was established to compete with the foreign banks and provide facilities for national savings. The National Investment Bank was established to cater for the financial needs of industrial enterprises; and so was the Agricultural Development Bank to provide the financial needs of the agricultural sector. Later the Capital Investment Bank undertook the promotion of investment in Ghana. It granted fiscal concessions and other incentives for approved investment and generally assisted would-be investors to establish projects in Ghana. Not withstanding these efforts, Ghana's financial problems worsened.

NOTES

1. Birmingham, W.; Neustadt, L. and Omaboe, E. N. (ed.) 1966. *Op. cit.*, p. 250.
2. Niculescu, Margaret 1957. *Op. cit.*
3. Gold Coast Colony 1944. *General Plan for the Development of the Gold Coast.* Accra: Government Printing Department.
4. ADM 1/2/272. Governor to Secretary of State for the Colonies. January 1940. G.C. No. 103 of 16/2/40; ADM 1/2/272. Joint Provincial Council

to Secretary of State for the Colonies. September 5, 1943; ADM 1/2/258 Saving Officer Administering the Government to Secretary of State for the Colonies. 10/2/46.
5. ADM 1/2/282. Saving Governor to Secretary of State for the Colonies. 26/1/46.
6. De Kun, Nicolas 1965. *Op. cit.*, p. 90; *West Africa*, October 1, 1949.
7. Kesse, G. O. 1981. Gold potentials of Ghana. *International Seminar on Ghana's Gold Endowment, 6 January, 1981.*
8. The Gold Coast Chamber of Mines 1950. *Op. cit.*, p. 24; Junner, N. R. 1973. *Op. cit.*, p. 5.
9. The Gold Coast Chamber of Mines 1941. *14th Annual Report of the Chamber for the Year Ended 31st May, 1941.*
10. ADM 1/2/272. Joint Provincial Council to the Secretary of State for the Colonies. September 1943; The Gold Coast Chamber of Mines 1946. *19th Annual Report, 31st March, 1946;* The Gold Coast Chamber of Mines 1950. *Op. cit.*, p. 25.
11. The Gold Coast Chamber of Mines 1946 and 1947. *19th and 20th Annual Reports, 31st March 1946 and 1947* respectively.
12. Culled from Appendix 1 of the *22nd Annual Report of the Chamber of Mines for the Year Ended 31st March, 1949.*
13. *West Africa*, May 21st, 1949; ADM 1/2/261, Governor of the Gold Coast to Secretary of State for the Colonies. G.C. No. 66 of 21/2/41.
14. Agbodeka, Francis 1977. *Achimota in the National Setting. A Unique Educational Experiment in West Africa*, pp. 61–62. Accra: Afram Publications.
15. ADM 1/2/266. Governor of the Gold Coast to Secretary of State for the Colonies. G.C. No. 183 of 15/6/42 and encl.
16. ADM 1/2/261. Governor of the Gold Coast to Secretary of State for the Colonies. G.C. No. 66 of 21/2/41.
17. Gold Coast Chamber of Mines 1949. *22nd Annual Report, 31st March, 1949.*
18. Myint, H. 1973. *Op. cit.*, p. 42.
19. Gold Coast Chamber of Mines 1949. *22nd Annual Report, 31st March, 1949.*
20. *West Africa*, October, 1949; *Report of the Mines Department on Mineral Industry for the Year 1945–1946;* Gold Coast Chamber of Mines 1950 *Op. cit.*, p. 24; *Legislative Council Debates Session 1945*, March 6th, 1945.
21. Gold Coast Chamber of Mines 1949. *17th Annual Report, 31st May, 1949;* Gold Coast Chamber of Mines 1950. *Op. cit.*, p.25.
22. *West Africa*, April 3rd 1949.
23. Greenstreet, Dennis, K. 1979. *Op. cit.*
24. Birmingham, W.; Neustadt, L. and Omaboe, E. N. (ed.) 1966. *Op. cit.*, p. 250.
25. De Kun, Nicolas 1965. *Op. cit.*, p. 443.
26. *Ibid.*, p. 91.

Towards a New Era 131

27. Birmingham, W.; Neustadt, L. and Omaboe, E. N. (ed.) 1966. *Op. cit.,* p. 266; De Kun, Nicolas 1965. *Op. cit.,* p. 443.
28. De Kun, Nicolas 1965. *Op. cit.,* p. 91.
29. Lawson, Rowena, M. 1957. *Op. cit.,*
30. *Legislative Council Debates Session 1945.* Issue No. 1, March 6th, 1945.
31. Birmingham, W.; Neustadt, L. and Omaboe, E. N. (ed.) 1966. *Op. cit.,* p. 266.
32. Gold Coast Chamber of Mines 1959. *32nd Annual Report, 31 st March, 1959,* Appendix p. 33; *West Africa,* October 1, 1949; *Legislative Council Debates Session 1945,* Issue No. 1, March 6th, 1945.
33. Gold Coast Chamber of Mines 1943 and 1945. *16th and 18th Annual Reports, 31st May, 1943 and 1945* respectively.
34. De Kun, Nicolas 1965. *Op. cit.,* p. 285.
35. Gold Coast Chamber of Mines 1976. *Ghana Mining Industry.* Accra.
36. Gold Coast Chamber of Mines 1946. *19th Annual Report 31st March, 1946.*
37. *West Africa,* October 1, 1949.
38. *Legislative Council Debates Session 1945.* Issue No. 1, March 6th, 1945; De Kun, Nicolas 1965. *Op. cit.,* p. 92
39. Lawson, Rowena, M. 1957. *Op. cit.*
40. Birmingham, W. Neustadt, L. and Omaboe, E. N. (ed.) 1966. *Op. cit.,* p. 272; De Kun, Nicolas 1965. *Op. cit.,* p. 92.
41. De Kun, Nicolas 1965. *Op. cit.,* pp. 92 and 302.
42. Jopp, Keith 1965. *The Story of Ghana's Volta River Project,* p. 5. Accra: Volta River Authority.
43. *Ibid,*
44. Gold Coast Chamber of Mines 1958. *31st Annual Report 31st March, 1958.*
45. Higher wages in Ghana were due to scarcity of labour and higher cost of living in a fast developing primary sector.
46. Gold Coast Chamber of Mines 1958. *31st Annual Report 31st March, 1958.*
47. *Ibid.*
48. *West Africa,* January 8th, 1949.
49. Jopp, Keith 1965. *Op. cit.,* p. 16.
50. Dickson, K. B. 1961. Road transport in Southern Ghana and Ashanti since 1950. *Transactions of the Historical Society of Ghana* v (i): 33—42.
51. *Ibid.*
52. ADM 1/2/268. Encl. in G.C. No. 262 of 12/9/42.
53. Dickson, K. B. 1961. *Op. cit.*
54. ADM 1/2/268. Encl. in G.C. No. 262 of 12/9/42.
55. *Legislative Council Debates Session 1941.* Issue No. 1, February, 1941.
56. Dickson, K. B. 1961. *Op. cit.*
57. ADM 1/2/268. Encl. in G.C. No. 262 of 12/9/42.
58. ADM 1/2/275. July—August 1944. G.C. No. 222 of 26/7/44.

59. *Legislative Council Debates Session 1941.* Issue No. 1, February, 1941.
60. ADM 1/2/275. July-August 1944. G.C. No. 222 of 26/7/44.
61. ADM 1/2/256. Governor to Secretary of State for the Colonies. February—April, 1940. G.C. No. 222 of 26/7/44.
62. Agbodeka, Francis 1972. *Ghana in the Twentieth Century,* p. 99 Accra: Ghana Universities Press.
63. ADM 1/2/275. July—August, 1944. G.C. No. 222 of 26/7/44.
64. Bourret, F. M. 1960. *Ghana: The Road to Independence, 1919—1957,* p. 210. London: Oxford University Press.
65. *Ibid.,* pp. 209—210.
66. *Ibid.,* p. 210.
67. ADM 1/2/258. Governor to Secretary of State for the Colonies. G.C. No. 430 of 28/8/40.
68. ADM 1/2/257. Governor to Secretary of State for the Colonies. April 1940, Encl. in G.C. No. 286 of 16/5/40.
69. ADM 1/2/258. Governor to Secretary of State for the Colonies. G.C. No. 430 of 28/8/40.
70. Birmingham, W.; Neustadt, L. and Omaboe, E. N. 1966. *Op. cit.,* p. 332.
71. *Ibid.,* p. 333
72. ADM 1/2/257. Governor to Secretary of State for the Colonies. April 1940. Encl. in G.C. No. 286 of 16/5/40.
73. ADM 1/2/256. Governor to Secretary of State for the Colonies. G.C. No. 209 of 10/4/40.
74. ADM 1/2/258. Governor to Secretary of State for the Colonies. G.C. No. 430 of 28/8/40.
75. ADM 1/2/272. 5th September, 1943 to 31st December, 1943.
76. Birmingham, W.; Neustadt, L. and Omaboe, E. N. (ed.) 1966. *Op. cit.,* p. 334.
77. The harm done in Ghana by multi-national companies is immense and deserves detailed study.
78. Birmingham, W.; Neustadt, L. and Omaboe, E. N. (ed.) 1966. *Op. cit.,* p. 380.
79. *Ibid,,* pp. 339—340.
80. *Ibid.,* p. 381.
81. *Ibid.,* p. 340.
82. **Greenstreet, Dennis, K. 1979.** *Op. cit.*
83. **Priestley, Margaret 1976.** *Ghana's Financial Bureaucracy: A Historical Approach. An Open Lecture Delivered at the University of Ghana, Legon.* **Accra: Ghana Universities Press.**
84. *Legislative Assembly Debates,* **11th February, 1953**
85. **Birmingham, W.; Neustadt, L. and Omaboe, E. N. (ed.) 1966. *Op., cit.,* pp. 305—308.**
86. *Legon Observer* II (ii), 26th May — 8th June, 1967.
87. *Legon Observer* I (6), 16th September, 1966.
88. *Legon Observer* II (ii), 26th May — 8th June, 1967.
89. ADM 1/2/299. Saving Governor to Secretary of State for the Colonies.

15th April, 1948.
90. ADM 1/2/303. Governor to Secretary of State for the Colonies. 29th September, 1948; Seers, Duddley, and Ross, C. R. 1952. *Op. cit.*, p. 25.
91. ADM 1/2/299. Saving Governor to Secretary of State for the Colonies. 15th April, 1948.
92. Seers, Duddley, and Ross, C. R. 1952. *Op. cit.*, p. 25.
93. *Legon Observer* I(6), 16th September, 1966.
94. *Legislative Council Debates 1946.* Issue No. 1, March 21st, 1946.
95. ADM 1/2/295. Officer Administering the Government to Secretary of State for the Colonies. 30/10/46.
96. ADM 1/2/295. Officer Administering the Government to Secretary of State for the Colonies. 15/11/49.

Chapter 8

TOWARDS A NEW ERA: INDUSTRIALIZATION

General
By the term industrialization we mean the establishment of secondary industries which involves mechanizing the processing of primary produce into finished or semi-finished goods. In this context, then, primary produce comes from agriculture, fishery, forestry and mining. So secondary industries would be the processing into finished or semi-finished goods of farm and forest produce, fish and minerals. Industrialization in our context means mechanizing a number of local industries nurtured manually in the above areas, by traditional methods since time immemorial. By the close of the 19th century they included salt-manufacture, pottery, boat-making, weaving, wood-working, carving and sculpture. Carpentary and joinery were introduced in the 19th century by missionaries who had to erect schools, churches, mission houses and offices.

Industrialization in the Pre-1950 Period
Throughout the first four decades of the 20th century, the manufacturing industries dragged on a chequered existence in the towns and villages of Ghana. Early missionary skill trickled into even the remotest villages and was left to be nurtured, by trial and error, during the period till a fairly-high standard of workmanship was attained, particularly in joinery, by about 1940.[1] Most other manufacturing industries, however, remained dwarfed until the Second World War when they began to pick up.

One of the main reasons for the depressed state of manufacturing industries in the earlier part of this century was lack of incentives. Relatively cheaper European imports since the opening years of the 20th century rendered laborious local manufactures highly uncompetitive. So, this put a brake on the improvement of traditional techniques. For example, imports of Manchester prints or those of cheap Japanese cotton goods in the 1930s adversely affected the weaving industry. United Kingdom salt imports into Ghana also weakened the local salt manufacturing industry. Equally damaging to the growth of manufacturing industries was the negative attitude of the colonial regime. In order to avoid local competition, the Colonial Administration did not adopt a policy of official encouragement of manufacturing.[2] Instead, it clamped down on local invention and talent and forbade the import of machinery to improve on local manufacturing techniques.[3] The greatest obstacle to progress in this respect, however, was that awareness that public enterprise was its responsibility dawned on government only very slowly and indeed it took World War II to sharpen official reaction to industrialization.[4]

But a number of developments ushered in a period of change. The first of these was African pressure for a change. In the 1930s, far-seeing African leaders asked for the strengthening of existing local manufacturing industries and introduction of new ones.[5] Indeed, they were so serious about this that in 1934 a Ghanaian delegation to the United Kingdom presented to the HM's Government a petition which in part read

> All profits made ... are taken back to Europe and other foreign countries ... The chief cause of this lies in the fact that the Gold Coast is mostly an exporting country, exporting raw materials, and the absence of any locally manufactured articles ... has placed the country in the unenviable position for the imports of other countries".[6]

A decade later in 1943 they were still arguing that without industrialization they, as a people, could not reach maximum development. In fact they no longer pleaded with government for small industries but wanted "as full a development of our industries"[7] as the country could afford.

This African pressure resulted in the strongest support yet for industrialization of Ghana before the 1950s. Governor Alan Burns was moved to seriously consider altering British policy on the Coast in this regard, and made plans towards effecting such a change.[8] But, of course, the plan itself did not go far enough and still gave the lion's share of development to primary, i.e. agricultural and extractive, industries before turning to a few local secondary manufacturing industries. Even so, the Governor's list of these local manufacturing industries was the most comprehensive ever and consisted of soap-making, furniture making, bricks and tiles and cloth-weaving.[9] He even went as far as suggesting a legislation to reserve the development of these manufacturing industries for African enterprise, but the competition from imported goods in peace time was so strong that it was felt that, with the end of the war in sight, African enterprise could not survive and the proposed legislation was accordingly dropped.[10]

The only other agent that independently promoted the cause of industrialization was Achimota which, in addition to a Department of Ceramics to improve local pottery,[11] established, with government support, an Institute of Arts, Industry and Social Science geared to modernizing local manufacturing industries in Ghana. Also because of the war and limited shipping space, there was need for local manufactures during the Second World War and so the Forestry Department of the Colonial Administration promoted the growth of a large local manufacturing industry.[12]

Limited though these plans were, they nevertheless constituted a ray of hope for the industrialization programme the educated Africans had in mind. But these hopes were shortlived. A strong opposition rose up against even this limited liberal approach to industrialization and manifested itself in an Economic Development Committee established by the Colonial Administration in 1945. They rejected the fostering of manufacturing industries and cut down the list of local manufacturing industries which should be officially recognised. Only furniture, weaving at Avatime and boots and shoes were left.[13] All others including sugar manufacture, so much advocated by Africans, were discouraged.[14] They suggested the establishment of an African Industries Bureau (AIB) to look after these manufacturing industries. But when the AIB was established, it turned out to be no more than a furniture depot. The other local manufacturing industries approved did not feature in the Bureau's work.[15]

Of the local manufacturing industries striving in the first half of the 20th century, wood-working, carpentary and joinery received the greatest attention. This manufacturing industry was built up at the village level and attained a high standard of workmanship by 1940. A large number of carpenters were to be seen all over the country producing furniture.[16] Indeed, throughout the 1930s, these carpenters were making furniture, doors and windows and wooden sleepers for the Ghana railway.[17]

It was not surprising, therefore, that with the outbreak of the Second World War a number of wood-workers quickly learnt how to produce many more wooden articles such as easy and stacking chairs, tables, trays, side-boards, bed ends, waste paper baskets, table lamps, standing lamps, etc., the majority of these for the Army and Air Force. It was clear that a manufacturing industry was gradually emerging out of the timber business.[18] A little effort (i.e. acquiring a small machine and a trainer) was all that was needed to modernize this industry to manufacture high class furniture for the export market.[19] But this was not done, even though this was clearly an area where no competition with British industrialists existed. The truth was that there was a competition with private saw mills, mainly in the Takoradi area, United Africa Company and the Public Works Department, all of which had begun by 1945 to produce furniture, taking advantage of their larger capital base to develop this industry on the achievements of the village craftsmen.[20] As we have already seen, government efforts at developing the recognized local manufacturing industries yielded no more than a furniture depot. Even the limited modernization or factory production recommended for only furniture works was side-tracked. Other cottage crafts from forest products included pole-cutting, wood carving, basket and cane chair weaving.[21]

Another cottage manufacturing industry which survived up to the Second World War was cloth-weaving, particularly in Avatime in the Volta Region, which had a traditional hand-spinning and weaving industry.[22] Avatime's achievements attracted Achimota College authorities and they planned to develop it through the agency of the Institute of Arts, Industry and Social Science. The Colonial Administration supported this because, as we have seen, the war made such developments necessary. But the Government's plan was of course not to promote a modern industrial establishment here but to encourage Avatime's cloth-weaving, only as a cottage industry.[23] As early as 1942, Mr. Southern of the Institute visited the Volta Region and surveyed the local textile industry and cotton growing there. His plan was to establish a strong cotton weaving industry at Achimota and thereafter extend the skill to Avatime. In July 1942, Mr. Southern established a Textile Unit at Achimota College. He also established a cotton breeding station at the College, and got broad looms to be built there.

Mr. Southern went back to the Volta Region and introduced the broad looms and got his Achimota staff to teach the local Avatime weavers how to use them. Local carpenters were instructed in making the looms. In October 1942, the Achimota College Textile Unit began to train textile apprentices. Mr. Southern and the Achimota authorities were of course enthusiasts in social and economic reform and proceeded to plan building an expanded Industrial Textile Unit. Already, the Unit was producing cloth for College uniforms, furnishings etc.[24] However, since it was never government's intention to see a modern industrial textile unit developing at Achimota or anywhere else in the country, it withdrew financial support for the project which languished when the needs of war were over.

Meanwhile, from 1943, the institution was instrumental in developing the weaving industry in Avatime. Seven broad looms and 40 spinning wheels were constructed by 1943 and training courses were begun for weavers from the southern part of the Volta Region.[25] The entire scheme for the Avatime towns consisted of making and distributing spinning wheels and looms, free distribution of cotton seeds to farmers there and purchase of yarn from spinners and courses of instruction to be given to spinners and weavers in the area. By 1944, more than 200 spinning wheels were distributed to women who could use them and who had already attended the spinning courses held at Kpandu, Amedzofe and Ho. Altogether, 35 looms were to be constructed. When the new spinning wheels and the new looms went into operation, weaving became much faster. Avatime weaving proved to be the ideal cottage industry that government wanted.[26]

Leather works were also pursued throughout the first half of the 20th century. The hides and skins prepared in the country found a ready market among local craftsmen producing sandals, sleeping mats, etc. This was the third manufacturing industry approved for government attention. But the government was content to leave the cottage leather industry to its fate. Local tanning had not developed properly, but the local Colonial Administration saw no need to lend its support to the efforts of the local craftsmen.

Gold-smithing also developed very rapidly when gold mining became firmly established in Ghana, particularly in Asante. Asante goldsmiths were, around 1940, making beautiful gold plates embodying in their designs various emblems.[27] This manufacturing industry survived the Second World War and was in fact, ushered into the post-independence period. Black-smithing, also an ancient cottage industry, staggered through the period, supplying the simple tools needed by the farmers. Imports of some of these tools like matchets tended to subvert this industry and even though the blacksmith could still be seen in the countryside, his methods remain crude and inefficient.

There were two manufacturing industries to which the Institute of Arts, Industry and Social Science paid particular attention. These were bricks and tiles and pottery. Bricks and tiles in fact owed their existence to the Institute. Pottery too, even though it was one of the earliest traditional crafts in the country, had new aspects developed by the Institute.[28]

In 1944, the Institute started an experimental factory at Alajo near Accra to produce units adapted for villages where they would be utilized for making bricks. These bricks were to be popularized as local building materials to solve the housing problem facing Ghana after the war. The Institute also set up units at Kpandu and Kumasi to make tiles. It hoped tile-making would expand from these centres to the countryside of Ghana and beyond.[29]

Pottery had, in Ghana, been a woman's occupation. Women in different parts of the country produced beautiful pots for various purposes. This craft has continued to our own day; but what the Institute did in 1944 was to introduce in Ghana glazed pottery as a new village or urban craft. Thus, alongside the part-time occupation of women, pottery also developed into full-time job for new specialists.[30]

Soap-making in Ghana emerges from antiquity. Made from wood-ash and vegetable oil, the traditional soap in the form of a "ball" has been popular with the greater part of the population. This was in fact the case even as late as the 1960s and 1970s. However, since the First World War, soap imports from Europe gradually increased. A few factories came into existence in Ghana before World War II to supply about half the pre-war imports of factory made soap.[31] The result was that energies which could have gone into improving the locally-made "ball" soap got expended on either imported European-made soap or locally factory-produced soap. Both, of course, depended on foreign inputs and, therefore, not the best development for the country. Serious soap shortages experienced in the late 1970s and early 1980s could be attributed to this development.

In the area of food-processing the oldest industry was palm oil extraction. This was the only oil seed which has never been exported raw, but always in the form of oil. Other oil seeds or oil-producing fruits including coconuts, groundnuts, palm kernel etc. also formed the basis of oil extraction industries, but they were often exported raw as well. Up to the Second World War not much was done to modernize the oil extraction business. Some hand-presses were introduced to improve the palm oil extraction technique since the 1920s but it was in the late 1940s that United Africa Company sponsored a serious effort to modernize palm oil extraction. But the traditional technique still exists in the villages. Throughout the first half of the 20th century the extraction of oil from the other seeds or fruits remained crude and ineffective. The processing of root crops has not been common, except that of cassava into gari. Here again, there has not been any spectacular improvement in techniques. The only changes which have occurred have to do with the first stages of the processing, i.e., the grinding of these products into powder form. In connection with this, different types of grinding mills have been introduced into Ghana. They are invaluable in the preservation process for a number of farm products.

Citrus fruits, as we have seen, grow well in the Central Region and elsewhere in Ghana, but their preservation has always been a problem. We discussed in Chapter 6 how, in the early 1920s, Messers L. Rose and Company Limited established a lime juice factory at Asebu in the Central Region, and how in the late 1930s the company extended the factory facilities. The result was that L. Rose and Company Limited now utilized larger quantities of lime for the production of lime products,[32] and thus nurtured a vibrant manufacturing industry throughout the 1940s and 1950s.

Apart from this venture in the Central Region, only a small unit existed at Achimota for the preservation of fruits. Achimota College had a farm producing, among other things, fruits and vegetables. Before the Second World War, a small fruit juice industry was established as part of the farm complex. During the war, the fruit juice industry became vital. In 1942, 8,000 bottles of juice were produced.[53]

The war also necessitated canning fish to preserve it, but like the Achimota enterprise the fish-canning factory at Osu closed down soon after the war.

Thus, by 1948 the number of local manufacturing industries that had any hopes of developing was indeed small. The future seemed to belong more to the growing number of Western-style factories[34] being established at this time, and the import system which might continue to monopolize the supply of most goods needed in Ghana.

Industrialization in the 1950s and 1960s

During the 1950s and 1960s, industrialization was regarded by the nationalists as the best way to develop Ghana. The reasons for this belief were several. The nationalists argued that it was through the establishment of manufacturing industries that the advanced countries achieved development. If Ghana set up manufacturing industries for import substitution and thereby processed some agricultural, forest and mining products, the country would earn foreign exchange, increase employment and productivity.[35] These developments would in turn minimize such economic evils like inflation and black marketing. Concentration on manufacturing industries was all the more necessary because with the fluctuations of agricultural produce prices on the world market no one could be certain of the future of agriculture for developing countries. Prices of industrial finished goods were more stable and this constituted an insurance for the future.[36] Industrialization was thus generally admitted to be the surest way of raising the standard of living of the people.[37]

Two schools of thought gave expression to two contrasting views about how best to go about industrializing Ghana. The Colonial Authorities in Ghana claimed that the only practicable framework for industrialization was within the local authority system. Development of manufacturing industries should be at the village and district levels. This was why they established, in 1949, local development committees in all districts with provision of funds to assist in the execution of small-scale manufacturing industries planned by the committees in accordance with local wishes.[38] An important reason for this development was that by the late 1940s, native authorities had blossomed into functional administrative units,[39] and to the British, always trying to lessen financial burden on the Central Government, it would be a pity not to utilize these local authorities.

Apart from the argument of practicability, there was the point that such a framework could only support small-scale manufacturing industries and there seemed to be no intention of the British authorities to go beyond small cottage manufacturing industries in most cases. This was borne out by their 'policy' for overall development, namely, that it was through agricultural exports that the country could develop social services and improve the standard of living generally. Heavy industrialization had no place in this programme at least not at the early stages.[40] Practical expression was given to this theory when the 1951 plan allocated, in effect, only a little over £1 million to industrial development proper, while £13 million, £10 million and £5 million went to education, local government and housing respectively.[41]

This interpretation of British policy had support in other quarters,[42] including Mc Kay, Colonial Affairs expert of Foreign Policy Associations, N.Y., who, however, maintained that this British approach to Ghana's development was not a malicious attempt to cheat the country, but was just due to the lack of a systematic plan of development on their part.[43] Other scholars also felt that, when since 1940, the United Kingdom Government accepted as their responsibility the task of promoting economic growth in colonial territories with a view to making an economic reality out of the granting of political independence at a later date,[44] they were sincere and this theory of development through agricultural exports was a genuine intention to help the colonies. Others like Arthur Lewis, who accepted this interpretation of British policy in pre-independent Ghana, were quick to point out that for it to work it should have been accompanied or at least followed by a deliberate attempt to build up African enterprise in the field of manufacturing.[45] As this was in fact not done, the field of manufacturing was left open for foreign entrepreneurs with little advantage to the country.

There was yet another group of scholars who were even more forthright in condemning British policy as one designed to support foreign commercial and industrial interests alone. They also accepted that after 1945 central planning emerged in Africa but it was mainly to set targets for export growth. It also produced shopping lists required for the construction of infrastructure for the export-oriented economy.[46] The last thing the United Kingdom authorities and the local Administration in Ghana wanted was heavy industrialization. Answers to questions on industrialization in the British House of Commons in 1946 were so vague as to lend support to this assertion.[47] The ban in 1946 on the export from Nigeria of the locally-woven Nigerian cloth, Adire, shows that it was a West African policy to clamp down on manufacturing industries that could compete effectively with British manufactures.[48] There can be no doubt that anything bigger than small-scale manufacturing industry did not meet with British official or private commercial approval. After all the Industrial Development Corporation established in Ghana (1947), with the birth of the central planning idea, sponsored nothing more than small manufacturing industries,[49] which in no way posed a threat to British industry.

The second school of thought was that of the educated Africans and it gave expression to the view that only large-scale industrialization could adequately meet Ghana's needs. They arrived at this conclusion because of the uncertain future of agricultural produce on the world market. Besides, they believed that a primary-produce-exporting country could not prosper as a manufacturing country which had the great advantage of accumulating the value-added of processed goods. To achieve large-scale manufacturing in Ghana it was felt, first, that the Volta River Project would be necessary; and secondly that public industrial corporations must be established.

The Volta River Project was in fact regarded, in the 7-Year Development Plan (1963—1970), as the keystone of Ghana's industrial development. It was accordingly the largest item of investment in the Plan. The Hydro-Electric Project alone was to cost £56 million.[50] Industrialization is faster where a country has minerals that lose weight on processing. Ghana has only one such mineral, i.e. bauxite, but in vast quantities,[51] and this could lead to a giant industrial establishment if cheap hydro-electric power could be used to smelt bauxite into alumina.[52]

Industrialization could also be favourable in consumer goods industries for the home market. This would depend on increased purchasing power in Ghana, which in turn depended on greater income through (a) an increase in agricultural productivity or (b) maintaining cocoa incomes at the pre-1960 levels or (c) the Volta River Project which would change the economic structure of the country, increasing incomes and having a multiplier effect on demand. The first alternative would be a very long process. The second was impossible in face of rapidly-falling world cocoa prices. So whatever the choice was, either a giant aluminium industry or consumer goods industries for the local market, the Volta River Project seemed the best alternative method in industrializing Ghana.[53]

The potentialities of a hydro-electric power dam on the Volta were known as early as 1915 by the Colonial Administration in Ghana, which must have realized the opportunities such a project could offer for British investment. Ghanaian nationalists, particularly Nkrumah, also regarded the Volta River Project as the cornerstone of the country's industrialization programme. It was to utilize two of Ghana's major resources, the Volta river and the Yenahin bauxite deposits, to generate hydro-electric power and to produce aluminium respectively. The hydro-electric power would be used to process local bauxite into alumina and smelt the alumina into aluminium. Both projects would have offshoots such as aluminium − related manufacturing industries, irrigation for improved agriculture, lake transport and inland fisheries. All these facilities would lead to a massive industrialization of Ghana. As for the multinationals, they actually derived great benefits from their participation in the scheme in the 60's. So why did the project take so long to materialize in spite of nationalist agitation for it?[54]

Apart from delay due to unfavourable circumstances such as the trade depression of the '30s and the outbreak of the Second World War, the main reason why the project delayed until the '60s was its high cost. The original plan of a twin-project was to cost £230 million in 1956. So the scheme was revised, without the local bauxite project, down to £130.7 million in 1959. Later the dam on the Volta at Akosombo alone was to cost £70 million and a smelter at Tema to process alumina from the West Indies was to cost £54 million. Nkrumah's Government got the US and the UK Governments, as well as the World Bank to finance the main hydro-electric project at Akosombo. The Volta Aluminium Company (VALCO) smelter was built by Kaiser Aluminium and Chemical Corporation and Reynolds Corporation both of the the USA with Kaiser controlling 90 per cent of the shares. Extra expenditure was incurred on the Accra-Tema railway and the Tema harbour and township which were all integral parts of the scheme.[55]

The need to establish public corporations had historical reasons. The new independent regime of Ghana met with capital flight and it was clear that they must adopt some extraordinary measures to attract capital for the huge industrial projects they meant to pursue. Establishment of public corporations was the most important measure to attract foreign investment. At the same time, there was the need for government to control the industrialization process, particularly since Ghana's economy was throughout the 1950s largely under alien domination. If government direction was absent, industrialization might turn out to benefit foreign investors rather than Ghana. It was again public corporations which could establish government control of industrialization. As early as 1947, the Ordinance which established the Industrial Development Corporation, amended in 1951, made it possible for the Government, through the Minister responsible, to interfere with the operations of the Corporation. This feature of public corporations was maintained by independent Ghana after 1957, precisely because it answered an important need of the times.[56]

Corporations were necessary because the majority of manufacturing industries established were heavy, such as the Volta Aluminium Project, Iron and Steel Project, heavy chemical industry, agricultural products processing, e.g. sugar, though a few light industries such as furniture, diamond polishing, shoe making etc. also existed.[57] A few of the light manufacturing industries belonged to Lebanese and Syrians. There was a supervisory body under which the corporations were grouped. From 1947–1957, it was Industrial Development Corporation, in 1958–1960 Development Secretariat, in 1961–1963 the Ministry of Light and Heavy Industries, in 1964–1966 State Enterprises Secretariat, 1968 to the present Ghana Industrial Holding Corporation (GIHOC). Before its liquidation, the Industrial Development Corporation supervised 13 public corporations or state manufacturing enterprises. The Ministry of Light and Heavy Industries and State Enterprises Secretariat each supervised 30.[58] Obviously, a contributive factor to the launching of a programme of heavy industrialization was that in the early 1950s there was sufficient capital generated locally to at least start the programme, even though it was realized that foreign capital would still be sought to complete it. Local sources of capital for industrial development as a whole was in 1951 mainly loans from the Cocoa Marketing Board, successor to West African Produce Control Board, which because of higher cocoa prices and consequent expansion of cocoa farms, had accumulated vast reserves.[59] Trade surpluses also provided handsome funds. Then, there were external sources such as grants from the Colonial Development and Welfare Fund and foreign loans of various types. A summary of sources for financing the 10-Year Development Plan 1951–1961 is presented in Table 6.

TABLE 6

Sources for Financing the Ghana 10-Year Development Plan 1951–1961

	£
Transfer from surplus balances	7,500,000
Grants from CDWF	3,000,000
Loan to HM Government	800,000
Contribution from Revenue to 1955	7,100,000
Additional Export Duty on Cocoa to 1955	14,500,000
Loans from various sources	5,000,000
Total	37,900,000[60]

With these sources available for industrialization, the Industrial Development Corporation's methods consisted mainly of disbursing funds to various development agencies. By March 1954, the Industrial Development Corporation had given out loans totalling £65,078.[61] The Industrial Development Corporation also took over a few industries itself. Before 1957, it had taken over Warababa Industries at Nsawam, Isaac Brothers Laundry, and Nkawkaw sawmills.[62] Later in the 1960s, the other public holding corporations also adopted similar methods of establishing industries, but their efforts yielded no dividends. During the 1950s and 1960s, the nationalists had not yet fully realized the grave disabilities of grammar school type of education established by the British in the country. The paucity of technical education meant that education for skills and competence which was the bed-rock of industrial and technical development of a new nation was almost non-existent. The other short-coming already discussed was the fact that cottage manufacturing industries had declined before the 1940s and the war-period revival proved shortlived. Consequently, there was no store of industrial experience from African entrepreneurship that could be brought to bear on the new ventures of the Industrial Development Corporation. In particular, no managerial assistance was given to the beneficiaries of the loans disbursed. So, loans were issued to inexperienced recipients without attention to how the money was spent. In some cases, the loans were not being paid back and yet more loans were issued to these same companies. The Industrial Development Corporation showed gross inefficiency. Machinery was ordered without regard to how they could be used.

In the absence of African expert initiative in matters of industrialization, it was expatriates who advised the African Minister of Commerce and Industries on the operation of the state corporations. They advised the Minister on lines which benefited their own countries by leaving the field free for expatriate manufacturing industries. Consequently, the Industrial Development Corporation under the Ministry failed to promote indigenous businesses. A classic example was that Avatime weavers approached the Ministry of Commerce and Industries for assistance but the Ministry refused. The result was that a number of European firms took the kente cloth to Europe where they imitated it and brought the product back to Ghanaians to buy.[64] Besides, all private businesses taken over by the Corporation collapsed. True, the advice given by foreign consultants was that the new Ghanaian Administration should start with small industries to generate funds before embarking on heavy industries, but the insistence of the expatriate advisers on importing raw materials from Europe and the consequent collapse of these industries did not augur well for the acceptance of this advice. The Ghana Government under Nkrumah ignored it and went ahead with heavy industrialization for which heavy machinery and or the raw materials certainly had to come from outside.[65] Some of the heavy manufacturing industries established by the early 1950s included chocolate manufacture, vegetable oil milling; later textiles and shoe making became important. Brewing, tobacco manufacture, fruit canning and cement manufacture were also begun.

Some features of the industrialization programme worked against its success. If African enterprises, i.e. small manufacturing industries, had been promoted, the programme would have permitted maximum local input of raw materials, capital, managerial and technical skills and thus reduce the foreign exchange components of costs. The establishment of heavy manufacturing industries meant heavy reliance on foreign inputs but the manufactured goods could only be marketed locally and not in any hard currency area of the industrialized world. So the industries generated no foreign exchange to pay for the foreign inputs.[66]

To minimize dependence on Western technical experts and reduce foreign control of the industrialization programme, Dr. Kwame Nkrumah got the Cocoa Marketing Board to start the crash programme of sending students abroad for technical training in the 1950s. But the products of this scheme were not enough for the rapidly-growing number of factories in the country.[67]

Kwame Nkrumah's pursuit of industrialization in the 1950s was far from vigorous partly because he put all his hopes on the future Volta River Project as the surest way to success. But it was in this very project that the multinationals got Ghana entangled with the unfavourable VALCO Agreement, the worst feature of which was the neglect of the development of the local bauxite deposits. Plans to use hydro-electric power to smelt bauxite from Yenahin and Mpraeso into alumina as well as in an alumina-reducing-process formed the core of Nkrumah's industrialization programme for Ghana. Replacing the first stage with imported alumina, thus neglecting the development of the 230 million tonne local bauxite deposits, as VALCO did, constituted a total failure of Ghana's industrialization programme in the 1960s.[68]

The multinational companies did more. Quite often, it was British officials who in the 1950s suggested industrialization with the view to controlling it. British companies gave the African middle classes inducements by moving out of commerce gradually in favour of Ghanaians but they went into industrialization by establishing subsidiaries of their parent companies in Ghana. It was for these subsidiaries that British official influence in Ghana during the 1950s ensured favourable investment codes. Thus, the African middle classes were turning to trade and commerce instead of industrialization, or were busy pursuing the political kingdom with the mistaken hope that all other things would follow.

The use of public corporations, of which there were 47 in 1965, as a means of industrializing Ghana, no matter what merits they had, brought political interference and corruption into the public manufacturing programmes. This was because public corporations became secret wings of political parties. The majority in Parliament appointed the Chairmen of these corporations and so party political pressure was piled on the corporations. So, the top officials of these corporations were not dedicated to making the economic venture a success. The lower ranks followed suit and most corporations went into the red.[69]

The earlier corporations under the Colonial Government direction, apart from poor performance, had no intention of establishing heavy manufacturing industries. Later, under nationalist direction, they aimed at establishing heavy manufacturing industries but mismanaged the entire venture. There are accounts of managerial ineptness and administrative bungling. Corruption and nepotism became increasingly widespread. Some corporations had, by 1965, accumulated losses nearly equal to their original capital fund.[70]

By the close of the 1960s, therefore, the manufacturing industries in Ghana were not working well and yet the country had incurred huge foreign debts on account of them. International debt, in the early 1970s, amounted to £200 million.[1] Thus, instead of retaining economic surplus for local use in Ghana, industrialization rather landed Ghana in debt.

NOTES

1. ADM 1/2/268. Encl. in G.C. No. 346 of 15/12/42.
2. Apter, David, E. 1972. *Ghana in Transition*, p. 74. Princeton University Press.
3. La Anyane, S. 1963. *Op. cit.*, p. 145. The local manufacture of spirits, for instance, was made illegal and imports of spirits went up at the same time.
4. ADM. 1/2/272. 5th September, 1943 to 31st December, 1943.
5. Apter, David, E. 1972. *Op. cit.*, p. 74.
6. La Anyane, S. 1963. *Op. cit.*, p. 193.
7. ADM 1/2/272. 5th September, 1943 to 31st December, 1943.
8. *Ibid.*
9. Gold Coast Colony 1944. *General Plan for Development in the Gold Coast.* Accra: Government Printing Press.

10. ADM 1/2/279. G.C. No. 171 of 9/6/45.
11. ADM 1/2/262. Encl. in G.C. No. 160 of 5/6/41.
12. ADM 1/2/273. January 1944 – April 1944.
13. ADM 1/2/279. Encl. in G.C. No. 171 of 9/6/45.
14. ADM 1/2/285. Saving Officer Administering the Government to Secretary of State for the Colonies. 18/9/41.
15. ADM 1/2/286. Saving Officer Administering the Government to Secretary of State for the Colonies. 13/11/46.
16. ADM 1/2/279. G.C. No. 171 of 9/6/45.
17. ADM 1/2/275. G.C. No. 222 of 26/7/44.
18. ADM 1/2/268. G.C. No. 346 of 15/12/42 & Encl.
19. ADM 1/2/279. G.C. No. 171 of 9/6/45 & Encl.
20. *Ibid.*
21. ADM 1/2/273, January 1944 to April 1944.
22. *Ibid.*
23. ADM 1/2/279. Encl. in G.C. No. 171 of 9/6/45.
24. ADM 1/2/269. Encl. G.C. No. 55 of 19/6/43.
25. ADM 1/2/271. G.C. No. 218 of 31/7/43.
26. ADM 1/2/273. January 1944 – April 1944.
27. ADM 1/2/255. Encl. in G.C. No. 90 of 9/2/40.
28. ADM 1/2/273. January 1944 – April 1944.
29. *Ibid.*
30. *Ibid.*
31. ADM 1/2/279. Encl. in G.C. No. 171 of 9/6/45.
32. ADM 1/2/255. No. 5 of 5th January, 1940.
33. Agbodeka, Francis 1977. *Op. cit.*, p. 104.
34. ADM 1/2/299. Governor to Secretary of State for the Colonies. 17th April, 1948.
35. Ghana 1963. *Seven Year Development Plan.* Accra: Office of Planning Commission.
36. Lewis, W. A. 1953. *Report on Industrialization and the Gold Coast.* Accra: Government Printing Department.
37. *West Africa,* November 2, 1946.
38. Gold Coast 1951. *The Development Plan.*
39. *Legislative Council Debates Session 1947.* Issue No. 1, March 18th 1947.
40. Gold Coast Colony 1948. *Op. cit.*
41. *Gold Coast Legislative Assembly Debates.* 10th February, 1953.
42. Lewis, W. A. 1953. *Op. cit.*
43. ADM 1/2/292. Saving Officer Administering the Government to Secretary of State for the Colonies. 2/8/47.
44. Niculescu, Margaret 1957. *Op. cit.*
45. Lewis, W. A. 1953. *Op. cit.*
46. Collins, Paul, D. 1978. Public sector mangement for development: An Overview. *School of Administration, University of Ghana Working Paper Series* 78(1): pp. 1–71.

47. *West Africa*, November 2, 1946.
48. *West Africa*, October 19, 1946.
49. Gold Coast 1951. *The Development Plan.*
50. Ghana 1963. *Seven Year Development Plan.* Accra: Office of Planning Commission.
51. Lawson, Rowena, M. 1957. *Op. cit.*
52. Adjei, K. E. 1977. State corporations in Ghana. Their performance and prospects. *School of Administration, University of Ghana Working Paper Series* 77: pp. 1–36.
53. Lawson, Rowena, M. 1957. *Op. cit.*
54. ADM 1/2/291. Saving Governor to Secretary of State for the Colonies. 15/7/47.
55. Jopp, Keith 1965. *Op. cit.*, Gold Coast 1951. *The Development Plan.*
56. Adjei, K. E. 1977. *Op. cit.*
57. Genoud, Roger 1969. *Nationalism and Economic Development in Ghana*, p. 62. New York: Praegar.
58. Greenstreet, Denis, K. 1979. *Op. cit.*
59. *West Africa*, July 23rd, 1949.
60. Gold Coast 1951. *The Development Plan.*
61. *Parliamentary Debates Session 1957–1958*, vol. 6, 23/4/57 – 12/7/57.
62. *Parliamentary Debates Session 1957–1958*, vol. 6, 6th June,
62. *Parliamentary Debates Session 1957–1958*, vol. 6, 6th June, 1957.
63. Adjei, K. E. 1977. *Op. cit.*
64. *Parliamentary Debates Session 1957–1958*, vol. 6, 6th June, 1957.
65. *Ibid.;* Ghana 1963. *Op. cit.*
66. Agbodeka, Francis 1986. *Op. cit.*
67. *Ibid.*
68. Birmingham, W.; Neustadt, L. and Omaboe, E. N. (ed.) 1966. *Op. cit.*,
69. Agbodeka, Francis 1986. *Op. cit.*
70. Guyer, David 1970 *Op. cit.*, p. 88.
71. Mountjoy, Alan 1982. *Industrialization and Developing Countries*, p. 142. London: Hutchinson.

Chapter 9

TOWARDS A NEW ERA: TRENDS AND PROSPECTS

General

Between 1966 and 1981, Ghana experienced political instability, with as much as six changes in government. This has resulted in stunted growth of the economy and in the first quarter of 1982 industrial production almost ground to a halt. Furthermore, lack of inputs hampered resumption of economic activity. Between 1974 and 1981 real Gross Domestic Product declined by as much as 15 per cent.[1]

Industrialization

Even before the 1966 coup d'etat, which brought about a number of changes into Ghana's economic and political life, the realization had dawned on the Nkrumah regime that, inspite of its commitment to establishing heavy manufacturing industries, cottage manufacturing industries should not be totally neglected. All along, therefore, some cottage manufacturing industries had been nurtured, even though the resources were geared more to large factories. When the coup came, most of the manufacturing industries, both cottage and large-scale, were abandoned. The First Military Administration reviewed these industries and decided to dispose of some of the large public enterprises, with the view to reducing government's financial commitments in the manufacturing sector.[2] Full state ownership and operation of the large corporations had resulted in heavy financial losses and it was natural for the National Liberation Council to shun full state participation in heavy industrial concerns as before.

Even though Ghana's foreign exchange problems had come during the course of industrialization, it was realized nevertheless that Ghana's hopes for a more prosperous era should be based on manufacturing industrial establishments. So, the First Military Regime and the Progress Party Administration could not ignore them. Probably, foreign control of Ghana's industrialization programme was its worst feature. Most of the manufacturing industries were even foreign owned. This was why both the Progress Party Government and the Second Military Administration (Supreme Military Council) were keen on putting more economic activity in the hands of Ghanaians.[3] So in 1975, the

Ghana Investment Policy Decree was promulgated,[4] to speed up the process of indigenization of manufacturing industries in Ghana. In order to avoid the pitfalls of the 1960s, the state had to check foreign control by participating in manufacturing industries but at the same time curb excessive financial commitments by avoiding full participation. This meant many joint-enterprises. In 1972, the Government acquired a controlling interest in Veneer and Lumber Company from the East Asiatic Company of Denmark, and Loyalty Group of Companies was acquired. In 1978, the assets of Fatal Vehicle Assembly (Ghana) Limited were transferred to the state. A number of manufacturing projects, abandoned following the 1966 coup d'etat, were reactivated under the Supreme Military Council (1972–1979). They included the Pre-fabricated Large Panel Factory, Tarkwa Gold Refinery, Aveyime Tannery and Tema Food Complex. Others were cottage manufacturing industries such as Axim Coir Fibre, Half-Assini Coir Fibre, Denu Groundnut Processing, and Bobikuma Rattan factories. In all Ghana Industrial Holdings Corporation came to have 16 state-private enterprises and the Ministry of Industries oversaw government financial interest in these enterprises.[5]

Throughout the 1970s and early 1980s, however, the capacity utilization of the various factories were pretty low. In 1980, textile factories, for instance, utilized no more than 20.1 per cent of their installed capacity; in 1979 food processing used only 22.9 per cent. Production levels fell drastically. In 1974, 121.3 million metres of cloth were produced; in 1981 it was 30.5 million; in 1975 about 2,746,000 tonnes of toilet soap were made; in 1981 the figure came down to 1,019.000 tonnes.[6]

In the 1950s, the nationalists looked at structural change in the economy merely in terms of ultimate results, namely industrialization, which would change Ghana from being a mere primary-produce-exporting and finished-goods-importing country into a self-sufficient and self-generating economy. Not much thought went into the ways and means of attaining the desired goal. But events of 1950s, 1960s and 1970s revealed that the method of achieving industrialization was just as important as the goal itself. Thus, the once-mentioned but largely ignored topics such as achieving diversified and efficient agriculture as a basis of industrialization, producing industrial raw materials locally, approaching industrialization cautiously through cottage and small-scale manufacturing industries, and using the local authority as a framework for developing the manufacturing industries tend, since the early 1980s, to be taken more seriously.

The National Liberation Council (1966–1970) and the Progress Party Government (1970–1972) had had no time to address themselves to these measures. The Supreme Military Council (1972–1979) paid attention to the first measures. Diversified and efficient agriculture was to provide alternatives to cocoa as export crops to minimize the ill-effects of a monoculture on the industrialization programme. It was also to produce enough food to feed an urbanized industrial society as well as release labour from the farms for the factories. Only a modest success was achieved. The other aspect of efficient agriculture was forest produce and the exports to be achieved in this area were to be as much as possible processed goods like veneer and lumber, wood works and handicrafts. This aspect is now being promoted by the present Provisional National Defence Council Government (1981–) through the Ghana International Furniture and Woodworking Industry Exhibition (GIFEX).

Growing industrial inputs locally will be dealt with under agriculture. The Provisional National Defence Council Government also attached great importance to using cottage and small-scale manufacturing industries as preparatory to heavy industrialization. In this regard, the PNDC Government has now reverted to the 1940 idea of using local units as framework for developing industries etc. The establishment of District Assemblies early 1989 has at last set up a local government machinery that would decentralize development. Instead of highly centralized economic activities of corporations with their unavoidable inefficiency, we now have small development units with greater chances of efficient operations.

Large public corporations have come to stay though. The PNDC realized this fact and, therefore, set itself the task of instilling financial discipline in the public sector and greater efficiency in operations of public corporations.[7]

Finding capital to pursue industrialization is important if success would come at last. Limann's Administration (1979–1981) had passed into law a very liberal Investment Code to attract foreign capital. At present the PNDC Government has gone in for International Monetary Fund and World Bank loans to develop several sectors of the economy.

Technical skill, so vital for industrialization, has to be acquired for a smooth industrial take off. A number of technical and vocational training institutes came up in different parts of the country, during the 1960s and 1970s. But technical education and training have not been streamlined. This has, therefore, been the main concern of the PNDC Government. In 1985, the Government turned to the National Vocational Training Institute, established since 1970, to co-ordinate vocational training in the country, to tackle the increasing problems of technical education and training. In addition it was decided to open Junior Secondary Schools (JSS) which would expose pupils to technical education and skills before they proceed to Senior Secondary Schools (SSS). The JSS started in 1987, merely exposes the pupils to the various skills but the NVTI actually trains the people for the various industrial projects.

Agriculture
Cocoa, as we have seen, is plagued with diseases. It was from 1956 that spraying cocoa trees against capsid and black pod attacks began. At the moment, concentration is on spraying against black pod, which has become a very serious cocoa disease. Apart from disease, lack of incentives led to decline in cocoa cultivation. From 1974 to 1982, there was a steady decline in production. In 1974, cocoa production was 385,100 tonnes; in 1981, it was 246,500 tonnes; and in 1982, further decline brought the figure down to 222,000 tonnes.[8] Since the crop is still the largest foreign exchange earner for Ghana, in spite of Ghana's fall to about the third or fourth place among the world's producing countries, everything is being done to resuscitate its cultivation. In 1981/82, the producer price of cocoa was raised from ₵120 to ₵360 per load of 30 kilogrammes. But even this failed to make an impact on production. A new system of paying the farmers by cheques to be deposited at the nearest banks rather than by cash has not helped either. Major rehabilitation programmes, started in Suhum in the Eastern Region have not as yet improved the long term prospects of recovery of the cocoa industry. In 1983, large cocoa farms were destroyed by bush fires and greater efforts are needed to achieve even a modest success in the recovery programme. Fluctuations of cocoa prices in the world market have continued to plague the industry.

It is precisely because of this that agricultural diversification is still being tackled, so that when cocoa prices fall, there would be other crops most probably with better prices and capable of bridging the country's financial gaps at the time. Limann's Government introduced some incentives so as to encourage coffee and shea nut farmers to expand their farms. In November 1981 the producer price of coffee was raised by 38.8 per cent and that of shea nut by 265.1 per cent. However, the Cocoa Marketing Board which looked after these two crops apart from cocoa had operational and logistic problems which affected the smooth production of these crops.[9] At present, there is an export drive involving not just these two, but also other crops like bananas, pineapples and ginger.

Diversification was also geared towards producing industrial raw materials locally. From the late 1970s, Government policy has been to encourage farmers to grow crops for the country's industries. So the production of cotton, oil palm, sugar cane and kenaf is on the increase. Food production also gains from agricultural diversification. By 1970, about 30 per cent of Ghana's population lived in the cities and had to be fed with food imported with foreign exchange earned from cocoa, gold, lumber and diamonds.[10] There was a drive to increase local food production. The Supreme Military Council had an early success with its food production programme (1972), but the resultant bumper harvests disappeared before the mid-1970s. Production of cereals and starchy staples went down; starchy staples from 7,990,000 tonnes in 1974 to 4,116,000 tonnes in 1981; cereals from 890,100 tonnes to 725,000 tonnes in the same period.[11] So, grains imports continued into the 1980s. This was what egged the PNDC Government on to a firm decision in 1982 to increase local food production. But in the same year, the rains failed to come and the following year saw bush fires all over the country causing havoc to many farms. In 1983, Ghana was struck by an accute shortage of food and essential commodities as was never before experienced in the country's history. Ghana's sufferings increased with the arrival of over 1 million returnees from Nigeria in this fateful year, 1983, adding so many more mouths to be fed. For diversification to succeed and increase agricultural produce for export, industry and food, there is a lot to be done about mechanization, seed improvement and multiplication, fertilizer, pesticides and particularly irrigation. Because of Ghana's great need in these three areas of economic activity something is being done right now about all these facilities, but much remains to be done. Irrigation in particular holds the key to the future of efficient farming practices; for as long as Ghana has to depend on the vagaries of the weather, crop failures and food shortages will continue.

Livestock breeding on the whole did not do badly during the 1970s. Indeed, poultry keeping improved. In 1975, fowls numbered 8,253,000 and in 1977 they numbered 13,560,000. Pigs increased from 270,000 to 569,000. Cattle, sheep and goats registered slight decline during the same period.[12]

Fishing also witnessed no dramatic changes. With the formation of the Volta Lake due to the hydro-electric dam at Akosombo, domestic catch was expected to rise. It did from 234,800 tonnes in 1976 to 262,100 tonnes in 1978, but there was a decrease to 224,100 tonnes in 1980. In the case of marine catch, it was the canoes which provided 77 per cent. Marine catch by trawlers declined steadily in the 1980s. Their problems were many. They lost their traditional fishing grounds with new definitions of territorial waters in West Africa; they had shortage of fishing nets, gear and spare parts.[13] These problems continued into the 1980s making the state-owned fishing corporation ineffective. Private fishing vessels seem to be doing better but only slightly. Even during the traditional bumper harvest months of August, September and October, the price of fish no longer goes down as much as before.

Forestry continues to be another important sector of the economy of Ghana. The difficulties of the timber industry consisting of corruption, lack of spare parts, haulage machines and other vital inputs, have left deep scars on Ghana's economy. The output of logs fell from 1.38 million cubic metres in 1976 to 0.48 million cubic metres in 1980. Similarly, the output of sawn timber fell from 0.45 million cubic metres to 0.15 million cubic metres during the same period. In the 1980s, the problem of corruption still threatens the industry's future, since even if funds, now available for an economic recovery programme, were sunk in reform, the foreign exchange deals and fraudulent transactions would not permit Ghana to reap the full benefits of these efforts.

Mining

In the 1970s, the production of the four main minerals declined. In 1975 and 1981, gold production was 16,295.1 kilogrammes and 10,595.3 kilogrammes respectively. Production of diamond was 2,336,200 carats and 836,100 carats, and that of bauxite 325,200 tonnes and 181,200 tonnes, while manganese production was 415,300 and 223,200 tonnes[14] in the same years. (See Fig. 8).

The prospects for mineral production are bright in the sense that their reserves are still very large and would last many more decades of mining. What is needed is capital to develop gold production beyond the 4 mines now operating, and to find new areas of diamond mining through the activities of the Birim Basin Project. Capital is needed to improve production of manganese oxide nodules of high metallurgical grade from the vast deposits of manganese carbonate at Nsuta, and to construct an alumina plant to process alumina from the bauxite deposits of Yenahin.[15]

Oil exploration has so far yielded nothing more than the modest output at Saltpond. In 1981, Phillips Petroleum Company indicated its wish to install a second drilling rig to speed up operations in off-shore oil prospecting. But there has recently been a slowing down of activities in this regard; and before substantial oil finds are made, a lot more capital needs to be sunk into exploration of hydro-carbons.

Construction

Naturally, with the financial crunch by 1966, subsequent Administrations could not embark on large-scale construction works. Even institutions like the Universities had their building programmes pruned down or postponed. Some projects commissioned in the 1960s are still unfinished today (1989). One project was, however, so vital to Ghana's existence that it could not be ignored or postponed. This was the Kpong Hydro-Electric Power Station which was constructed from 1977 to 1982. Also in the 1970s under the Acheampong regime, a great deal of private small projects such as residential houses took place. But decline in this construction activity came from 1981 as shortage of building materials, particularly cement, became acute. This activity is picking up only very slowly and has not as yet made any significant impact on the employment situation in the country.

Towards a New Era: Trends and Prospects 159

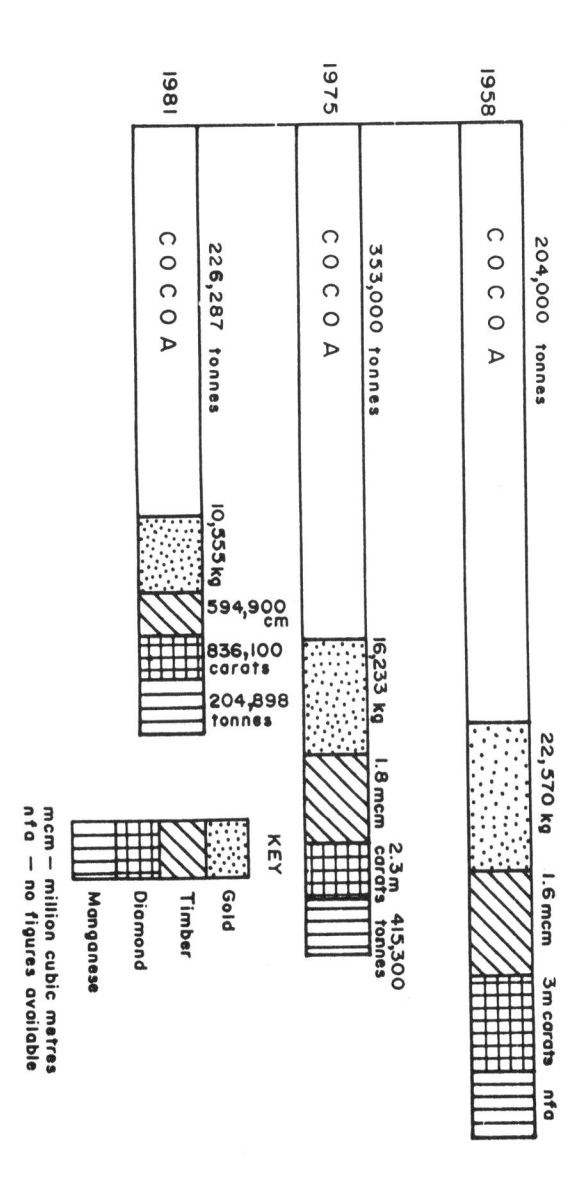

Fig. 8 Comparative Value of Ghana's Chief Exports in 1958, 1975 and 1981

Foreign Trade and Finance

We have already discussed the decline in production of the major exports of Ghana. Unfortunately for Ghana, this decline in the volume of cocoa, gold and timber was accompanied by an even sharper drop in the prices of these commodities on the world market, from the mid 1970s to the present. Export earnings fell from ₵3,458 million in 1980 to ₵2,924 million in 1981.

From the mid 1970s too, the cost of crude oil imported by Ghana was very high and in 1981 was actually 45.7 per cent of export earnings. This meant that not enough money was left for other essential commodities. Worst of all, the prices of these essential imports also rose very sharply and in 1981 reached ₵3,041.0 million. The combination of all these factors resulted in the acute shortages already referred to.[16]

Between 1974 and 1981, inflation rose at a terrific rate. President Limann's trade liberalization policy introduced by the end of 1980 in particular produced undesirable effects of black marketing and inflation. The PNDC Administration, in 1982, set itself the task of reducing the rate of inflation but the root cause was low productivity which is still prevalent in the various sectors of the economy. Inflation still has the upper hand. External debt rose from ₵436.4 million in 1974 to ₵4,100 million in 1981. With the procurement of International Monetary Fund loans Ghana's foreign debts are on the increase.

Ghana's efforts to enter a new era of industrialization seem to be fraught with more difficulties than those that attended similar changes in the pre-colonial period. We should note that the problems of economic change today are likely to be more clearly assessed, mainly because we now have faster means of communication, and developmental issues have now come under critical examination in a manner unknown to previous centuries. Having said that, we should hasten to add that economic development in our times indeed has unprecedented features. The first and most important feature is that the present efforts at self-development in Ghana received a rude shock; and these efforts were distorted by the long-term effects of colonialism. Briefly, colonialism has changed the cultural milieu in which 'natural' development takes place, making the people lose self-confidence. A host of undesirable effects accompany this cultural adulteration, rendering development much more difficult.

The content of development is the progressive application of science to change our environment. Ghana and indeed Africa lags behind in this, thanks to the break in our 'natural' development. It should, therefore, be more difficult to effect economic change today than in the pre-colonial period.

Furthermore, it is not just in the 20th century that Ghana experiences outside interference from multinationals. There was foreign interference in the economic affairs of pre-colonial Ghana. But this obstacle is greater today because of a teleguided middle class of Ghanaians that make it easier for outside forces to manipulate economic development even amidst nationalist slogans.

Since 1983

Above is a discussion of post-independence economic decline in Ghana up to 1983, with a summary of the reasons for this decline. Since 1983, and particularly from 1985, the reasons for decline have been analysed in greater detail. The negative effects of the colonial structure of the economy on Ghana's development have now been fully appreciated by scholars. Other reasons for decline include wrong policies such as the financial squeezing of the country's farmers and an over-valued cedi. There has been lack of appropriate technology for the nation's farmers.

Since 1983, these problems are being addressed in a manner that gives cause for optimism. There is an on-going revolution to restore Ghanaian cultural values and create the right atmosphere for the resumption of economic development.

The role of science in development is now fully recognized and technical education and training through the JSS (started in 1987) is now, as we have seen, being emphasized to give the nation the necessary scientific background. Together with practical experiences drawn from cottage and small-scale manufacturing industries, this would promote efficiency and productivity which may cause most of our economic woes to disappear.

Over-valuing of the cedi has given way to realistic exchange rates since 1987, and this is believed to be beneficial to local agricultural activities. Higher producer prices from 1985 have also helped to boost farming. In 1985, a target of 300,000 tonnes by 1991 was set for cocoa but is said to have already been reached in July 1989. Agricultural diversification has just been announced as having achieved an unprecedented 75 non-traditional exports in

1988. Under the Sasakawa Programme of Global 2000 (begun in 1988), featuring the Japanese philanthropist, Sasakawa, bringing help to small-scale farmers, Ghanaian farmers particularly in maize and sorghum have adopted new technologies that increase yields tremendously. Thus, food production seems to have a bright future in Ghana.

The Economic Recovery Programme (ERP) being pursued by the PNDC Government through IMF Structural Adjustment Programme, involving reduction in government expenditure and removal of subsidies, is designed to streamline economic activities, which must increase with IMF loans revitalizing industry and other productive ventures. Even though serious hardships result from these measures and the vast majority of the people have as yet not benefited from the ERP, the country has put in place (1989) a Programme of Action to Mitigate the Social Cost of Adjustment (PAMSCAD) to alleviate peoples' sufferings under the Structural Adjustment Programme. Furthermore, Economic Commision for Africa has already produced African Alternatives to the IMF Structural Adjustment Programme for African countries, which involves getting more for Third World raw material exports as well as processing more of these raw materials locally for value-added.

The efforts for change are promising, but to attain permanent success and for the benefits of change to reach down to the grassroots, the personnel involved in the process of change must be loyal to the cause of Ghana. From the 1950s, it was the teleguided middle classes or urban elite, who played this role. To orientate their thinking would be long and difficult. Decentralizing development can remove their influence more quickly. The establishment of District Assemblies in Ghana by the PNDC Government in the decentralization process should curb a teleguided middle class influence. Whether this will be achieved or not remains to be seen. If the middle classes remain powerful, the multinational companies would continue through them to drain the wealth of the toiling masses. But if scores of dedicated citizens emerge in the districts to use the better infrastructure being provided with external loans now coming in, Ghana can be ushered into a new era of industrialization and prosperity.

NOTES

1. Ewusi, Kodwo 1982. *The Ghana Economy in 1981–1982: Recent Trends and Prospects for the Future,* p.1. Accra: Institute of Statistical, Social and Economic Research, University of Ghana.
2. Greenstreet, Denis, K. 1979. *Op. cit.*
3. *Ibid.*
4. Collins, Paul, D. 1978. *Op. cit.*
5. Greenstreet, Denis, K. 1979. *Op. cit.*
6. Ewusi, Kodwo 1982. *Op. cit.,* p. 2.
7. *Ibid.*
8. *Ibid.,* pp. 2 and 40.
9. *Ibid.,* p. 8
10. Buchele, Wesley, F. 1969. *No Starving Billions: The Role of Agricultural Engineering in Economic Development. An Inaugural Lecture delivered on May 9th, 1969 at the University of Ghana, Legon,* Accra: Ghana Universities Press.
11. Ewusi, Kodwo 1982. *Op. cit.,* p. 2
12. *Ibid.,* p. 11.
13. *Ibid.,* p. 12.
14. *Ibid.,* p. 18.
15. *Ibid.,* p. 19.
16. *Ibid.,* p. 32.

POSSIBLE EXAMINATION QUESTIONS

Chapter 1

1. Analyze the conditions that favoured the emergence of agriculture in the tropical African forest around 500 BC.

2. What role did indigenous farm crops play in the expansion and establishment of agriculture in Ghana by about the first century AD?

3. Assess the importance of the knowledge and use of metals to the early economic development of Ghana.

4. In Ghana, "light and civilization came from the north". Explain this statement in terms of the early economic foundations of Ghana before the 15th century.

Chapter 2

1. In what ways did gold workings in Ghana revolutionize the country's economy in the 17th century?

2. Skill in crafts and trade is at the root of a country's prosperity. Examine the economy of 17th century Ghana in the light of this statement.

3. How do you explain the keen competition for the gold trade among the various European nations on the coast of Ghana?

4. Trace the development of Ghanaian coastal towns, emphasizing the major factors in their growth.

5. Examine the contributions of Timbuktu and Kano to the development of long distance trade between Ghana and the Western Sudan.

6. Describe the origins of Ghana's major cottage industries, assigning reasons for their rise.

7. Critically examine the link between the gold trade and Ghana's growing agricultural tradition in the 17th century.

8. Analyze the rapid development of farming practices and techniques in the Akwapem and Krobo districts of Ghana.

Chapter 3

1. Examine critically the origins of the Atlantic slave trade during the 15th and 16th centuries.

2. 'First a trickle, then a flood'. Is this an apt description of the expansion of the Atlantic slave trade?

3. Assess the significance of the major trade routes in Ghana to the expansion of the southern traffic up to the end of the 15th century.

4. How do you explain the paradox that the Atlantic slave trade stimulated the growth of certain traditional states in Ghana?

5. In what ways did the Atlantic slave trade affect Ghana's economy between 1750 and 1850?

Chapter 4

1. Discuss the origins and expansion of the oil palm industry in Ghana.

2. The 19th century was so full of promise and yet so scanty in achievements. Examine the state of either Ghana's agriculture or manufacturing industries during the 19th century in the light of this statement.

3. Describe efforts at Ghana's agricultural reform between 1830 and 1890.

4. The rubber industry was typical of Ghana's industrial development in the 19th century. Discuss this view.

5. Discuss briefly the pattern of local trade in 19th century Ghana.

6. Give an account of the development of transportation in Ghana during the 19th century.

7. Show how the technological base of Ghana's economy was either eroded or retarded during the 19th century.

8. Consider the claim that the 19th century was the turning point in Ghana's economic history and development.

Chapter 5

1. The replacement of indigenous with foreign technology and ownership of the mines in the 19th century, drastically reduced Ghana's benefits in both mineral and agricultural production during the 20th century. Explain.

2. What led to the decline in production of Ghana's export crops except cocoa by the first quarter of the 20th century?

3. Why was cocoa developed so dramatically into Ghana's leading export crop by 1911?

4. Why did Ghana fail to accumulate capital for financing industrial growth even though it was the world's leading cocoa exporter between the two World Wars?

5. Account for the continuing decline of manufacturing industries in Ghana throughout the first half of the 20th century.

6. Critically examine the statement that Ghana had the most highly developed peasant primary economy in Africa between the two World Wars.

7. Discuss the incidence of cocoa diseases and their effects on the cocoa industry in Ghana.

Chapter 6

1. Analyze the effects of the Second World War on the agricultural development of Ghana.

2. Attempt an appraisal of the Government's plans for agricultural development in the immediate post-war period in Ghana.

3. Why did the Government, in spite of its post-war plans for Ghana's agricultural development, slip back into its typical lukewarm approach to agricultural problems by 1948?

4. What other problems hindered the realization of Ghana's agricultural potentials in the 1950s?

5. Increased proceeds from agriculture in the 1950s had nothing to do with increased productivity or output on Ghana's farms. Discuss.

6. Why did Ghana's efforts to improve agriculture in the 1960s collapse?

7. Compare and contrast the factors responsible for the failure of the Ghana Government's agricultural programmes of the 'fifties with those of the 'sixties.

8. To what extent were the problems of Ghana's agricultural development in the '60s a continuation of those of the '50s?

9. Why and with what success were state farms established in the '60s?

10. Give an account of export crop development in Ghana during the 1960s.

11. Assess the efforts made in Ghana to increase food crop production from 1961–1965.

12. Examine the major features of timber production and export in Ghana during the twentieth century.

Chapter 7

1. Why was it misleading to use Ghana's export figures as an index of the country's wealth during the colonial period?

2. In a colonial territory, mineral and forest resources did not necessarily constitute the people's wealth. How true was this of Ghana's colonial economy?

3. Why was Ghana's colonial economy described as fragile?

4. How do you explain Ghana's economic crisis in the post-independence period?

5. Review Ghana's efforts in the '60s to benefit more from its mineral production, indicating why this goal could not be attained.

6. Give an account of road-building projects in southern Ghana up to 1957.

7. Examine the state of communications in Ghana during the decade following the Second World War.

8. Why was the balance of trade nearly always unfavourable to Ghana during the '60s?

9. Show how balance of payment deficits contributed to financial collapse in Ghana by the mid 'sixties.

10. Review the most disturbing features of the Ghanaian economy in the 'sixties and 'seventies.

Chapter 8

1. Examine the state of manufacturing industries in Ghana just before the Second World War.

2. Analyze the Ghana Government's attitude to industrialization during and after the Second World War.

3. Compare and contrast the Government's attitude to industrialization with that of Ghanaians, during the inter-war period.

4. Why did most Ghanaians enter commerce rather than industry in the '50s, in spite of the government's industrialization programme?

5. Why was the Volta River Project regarded as the king-pin of Ghana's industrialization programme in the '60s?

6. Events in the '50s robbed Ghana of experiences that might have been useful for industrialization in the '60s. Do you agree?

7. Why did President Nkrumah establish public corporations as part of his industrialization programme for Ghana?

8. Critically assess the role of multinational companies in Ghana's industrialization programme.

9. Attempt a critical appraisal of Ghana's industrialization policy of import substitution after independence.

10. The collapse of Ghana's industrialization programme in the 1960s was due to both internal and external factors. Discuss.

Chapter 9

1. How serious was agricultural decline in Ghana between 1975 and 1983?

2. Discuss the nature of the decline in mineral production in Ghana from the late 1960s.

3. What were the major financial problems facing Ghana between 1974 and 1981?

4. Critically examine the balance of payment problems of Ghana from the mid-'60s to the early '80s.

5. How would you describe Ghana's economic crisis in the '70s and '80s?

6. Review the effects of Ghana's economic crisis on its people?

7. How relevant were government measures to solve Ghana's economic problems between 1966 and 1979?

8. Attempt a critical appraisal of measures taken since 1985 to solve Ghana's economic problems.

BIBLIOGRAPHY

Primary Sources

Balme Library

West Africa, 1944–1949.

Report of the Committee of Enquiry on the Local Purchasing of Cocoa 1962.

Minutes of the Ashanti Farmers Association Limited, 1934–36 (ed. with introduction and notes by Kwame Arhin, March 1978)

The Gold Coast Cocoa Marketing Board 1952. *5th Annual Report for the Crop Year 1951/52.*

The Gold Coast Cocoa Marketing Board 1948. *1st Annual Report and Accounts for the year ended 30th September, 1948.*

The Ghana Cocoa Marketing Board 1957. *10th Annual Report for Crop Year 1956/57.*

The Ghana Cocoa Marketing Board 1954. *7th Annual Report for Crop Year 1953/54.*

Gold Coast 1951. *The Development Plan, 1951.*

Ghana 1963. *Seven Year Development Plan 1963.*

Gold Coast Colony 1931. *Report on the Eastern Province for the Year 1930–31.* Accra: Government Printer.

Annual Report on the Social and Economic Progress of the People of the Gold Coast 1931–32. Accra: Government Printer.

Republic of Ghana 1964. *Economic Survey presented to the National Assembly by the President.* Accra: Central Bureau of Statistics.

Gold Coast. *Annual General Report for the period 1st. April, 1930 to 31st March, 1931.*

Annual Report on the Eastern Province of Ashanti for the year 1930–31. Accra: Government Printer.

Legon Observer I(6). 16th September, 1966.

Legon Observer II(I). 6–19 January, 1967.

Legon Observer II(II). 26th May – 8th June, 1967.

Report of Fact-Finding Committee appointed by Ministry of Commerce, Industry and Mines, 1953.

Report of the Mines Department on Mineral Industry for the year 1945–1946.

Niculescu, Margaret 1957. *Report on Industrialization in the Gold Coast Today with Special Reference to Rural Areas.* Prepared for International Social Council, Paris.

Seers, Duddley and Ross, C. R. 1952. *Report on Financial and Physical Problems of Development in the Gold Coast.* Accra: Office of the Government Statistician.

Rouch, Jean 1954. *Notes on Migrations into the Gold Coast. 1st Report of the Mission carried out in the Gold Coast from March to December, 1954.* From CNRS, Paris: Mise de L'Homme.

Lewis, W. A. 1953. *Report on Industrialization and the Gold Coast.* Accra: Government Printing Department.

Chamber of Mines

The Gold Coast Chamber of Mines 1950. *Gold from the Gold Coast.*

The Gold Coast Chamber of Mines *14th Annual Report of the Chamber for the year ended 31st May, 1941. Annual Report, 31st March, 1959. Annual Reports 1960–1978.*

Ghana National Archives

ADM 1/2/200–295.

Legislative Council Debates Session 1945, March 1945.

Parliamentary Debates Session 1957–1958, Vol. 6, 23/7/57 – 12/7/57, 7th **June, 1957.**

Gold Coast Colony. *Legislative Council Debates 1946.* Issue No. 1, Session 1947 — March 18th, 1947.

Legislative Assembly Debates, 10th, 11th February, 1953.

Government of the Gold Coast 1919. *Report on Agriculture Department for the year 1918.* Accra: Gold Coast Press.

Gold Coast Colony 1932. *Agriculture Department Report, 1932.*

Gold Coast Colony 1944. *General Plan for Development in the Gold Coast.* Accra: Government Printer.

Nigerian National Archives

NA ICE/N3 Cmd. 5845 *Report of the Commission on the Marketing of West African Cocoa.* HMS Office, 1938.

Annual Report of the Registrar of Co-operative Societies for the period 1st July, 1967 to 30th June, 1968.

University of Ibadan Library

Gold Coast Colony 1947. *Report of the Department of Agriculture for the Year 1946—47.* Accra: The Government Printer, Government Printing Office.

Gold Coast Colony 1931. *Report of the Department of Agriculture for the Year 1930—31.* Accra: Government Printer.

Annual Report of the Department of Agriculture for the Period 1st April, 1954 to 31st March, 1955.

Gold Coast Colony 1948. *Report of the Department of Agriculture for the Year 1947—48.* Accra: Government Printing Office.

Secondary Sources

Books

Agbodeka, Francis 1972. *Ghana in the Twentieth Century.* Accra: Ghana Universities Press.

Agbodeka, Francis 1977. *Achimota in the National Setting. A Unique Educational Experiment in West Africa.* Accra: Afram Publications.

Apter, David, E. 1972. *Ghana in Transition.* Princeton: Princeton University Press.

Austen, Ralph 1987. *African Economic History.* London: James Currey.

Brimingham, Walter; Neustadt, L. and Omaboe, E. N. (ed.) 1966. *A Study of Contemporary Ghana. Vol. 1: The Economy of Ghana.* London: Allen and Unwin Ltd.

Bourret, F. M. 1960. *Ghana: The Road to Independence, 1919–1957.* London: Oxford University Press.

Chamber of Mines 1976. *Ghana Mining Industry.* Accra: The Chamber.

Davies, O. 1961. *Archaeology in Ghana.* London: Thomas Nelson.

De Kun, Nicolas 1965. *The Mineral Resources of Africa.* New York: Elsevier Publishing Company.

Ekundare, R. O. 1973. *An Economic History of Nigeria.* London: Methuen.

Ewusi, Kodwo 1982. *The Ghana Economy in 1981–1982: Recent Trends and Prospects for the Future.* Legon: ISSER University of Ghana.

Genoud, Roger 1969. *Nationalism and Economic Development in Ghana.* New York: Praegar.

Guyer, David 1970. *Ghana and the Ivory Coast: The Impact of Colonialism in an African Setting.* New York: New York University.

Hopkins, A. G. 1973. *An Economic History of West Africa.* London: Longman.

Junner, N. R. 1973. *Gold in the Gold Coast. Ghana Geological Survey Department Memoir, No. 4.* Ghana Publishing Corporation.

Jopp, Keith 1965. *The Story of Ghana's Volta River Project.* Accra: Volta River Authority.

La Anyane, S. 1963. *Ghana Agriculture. Its Economic Development from Early Times to the Middle of the Twentieth Century.* London: Oxford University Press.

Myint, H. 1973. *The Economics of the Developing Countries.* London: Hutchison.

Mountjoy, Alan 1982. *Industrialization and Developing Countries.* London: Hutchison.

Miracle, Marvin, P. and Seidman, Ann 1968. *State Farms in Ghana.* Madison: University of Wisconson.

The Gold Coast Chamber of Mines 1950. *Gold from the Gold Coast.* Accra: The Chamber.

Van Dantzig, Albert 1980. *Forts and Castles of Ghana.* Accra: Sedco Publishing Co. Ltd.

Articles

Adjei, K. E. 1977. State Corporations in Ghana: Their performance and prospects. *School of Administration, University of Ghana Working Paper Series.* 77: 1–36.

Agbodeka, Francis 1986. The roots of our present economic woes. 22nd. Inaugural Lecture, University of Benin, Benin City, Nigeria. Unpublished

Bevin, H. J. 1956. The Gold Coast Economy about 1830. *Transactions of the Gold Coast and Togoland Historical Society.* II(II): pp. 73–86.

Boahen, Adu 1961. Ghana Kola Trade. *Ghana Notes and Queries* 1: 8–10.

Boateng, E. A. 1957. The Tarkwa Gold Mining Industry – A Retrospect. *Bulletin of the Gold Coast Geographical Association* II(I): 5–9.

Buchele, Wesley, F. 1969. No starving billions: The role of Agriculture Engineering in Economic Development. An Inaugural Lecture delivered on May 9th 1969, at the University of Ghana.

Collins, Paul, D. 1978. Public Sector Management for Development: An Overview. *School of Administration, University of Ghana Working Paper Series* 78(I): 1–71.

Daaku, K. Y. 1961. Pre-European Currencies of West Africa and Western Sudan. *Ghana Notes and Queries* 2: 12–14.

Danquah, Moses 1958. The Saga of the Kente and how it is worn. *The Ghanaian* (3): 24, 25, 38.

Davies, O. 1958. Earliest man and how he reached Ghana. *Universitas* 35–37.

Davies, O. 1960. The neolithic revolution in tropical Africa. *Transactions of the Historical Society of Ghana* iv(ii): 4–20.

Dickson, K. B. 1961. Road Transport in Southern Ghana and Ashanti since 1650. *Transactions of the Historical Society of Ghana* V(II): 33–42.

Dickson, K. B. 1963. Origin of Ghana's Cocoa Industry. *Ghana Notes and Queries* 5: 4–9.

Greenstreet, Denis, K. 1979. The Growth of Public Enterprise in Ghana. *School of Administration, University of Ghana Working Paper Series* 79: 1–50.

Hill, Polly 1959. The History of the Migration of Ghana Cocoa Farmers. *Transactions of the Historical Society of Ghana* V(I): 14–28.

Kea, R. A. 1969. Akwamu-Anlo Relations, c. 1750–1813. *Transactions of the Historical Society of Ghana* X: 29–63.

Kea, R. A. 1970. Osei Kwame's Interdiction on Danish Trade 1788–89. *Ghana Notes and Queries* II(II): 36–41.

Kleist, A. M. 1957. The English African trade under the Tudors. *Transactions of the Historical Society of Ghana* II(II): 137–150.

Kesse, G. O. 1981. Gold potentials of Ghana. *International Seminar on Ghana's Gold Endowment, 6th January 1981.*

Kwamena-Poh, M. A. 1975. The traditional informal system of education in pre-colonial Ghana. *Presence Africaine.* 95: 269–283.

Lawson, Rowena, M. 1957. Ghana in economic transition. *The South African Journal of Economics* 25: 103–114.

Penfold, D. A. 1971. Excavation of an iron-smelting site at Cape Coast. *Transactions of the Historical Society of Ghana* XII: 1–15.

Priestley, Margaret 1976. *Ghana's Financial Bureaucracy: A Historical Approach. An Open Lecture delivered at the University of Ghana, Legon, on Thursday, 4th December, 1975.* Accra: Ghana Universities Press.

Rodney, Walter 1969. Gold and slaves on the Gold Coast. *Transactions of the Historical Society of Ghana* X: 13–28.

Swanzy, Henry 1956. A Trading Family in the 19th century Gold Coast. *Transactions of the Gold Coast and Togoland Historical Society* II(II): 87–117.

Southall, Roger, J. 1975. Polarisation and dependence in Gold Coast trade 1890–1938. *Transactions of the Historical Society of Ghana* XV(1): 93–115.

Van Dantzig, A. 1973. The Ankobra Gold Interest. *Transactions of the Historical Society of Ghana* XIV(2): 169–185.

Wilks, Ivor 1961. The northern factor in Ashanti history: Begho and the Mande. *Journal of African History* II(1): 25–34.

Wrigley, C. 1960. Speculations on the economic pre-history of Africa. *Journal of African History* I(2): 189–203.

INDEX

Aburi Botanical Gardens, 39, 57, 71
Accra, 12, 32, 33, 49, 51, 69, 100, 103, 120, 121, 131, 132, 149, 150, 163, 166, 169
Achimota College, 108, 137, 140
Ada, 28, 31, 32, 49, 52, 93
Agriculture, 15, 21, 22, 34, 36–39, 40, 54, 58, 59, 64, 65, 71, 72, 73, 74, 77, 79, 80, 81, 89, 168
  problems of, 75, 76
  Ministry of, 80
Agriculture Department, 66, 69, 75–78, 82, 87, 89, 91, 92, 166
Agricultural and Commercial Society, 62
Agricultural Development Corporation, 74, 79, 80, 82
Akan, 6, 10, 11, 16, 27, 34, 35, 106
Akwamu-Anlo relations, 28, 36, 168
Akwapem, 22, 39, 40, 42, 45, 46, 49, 56, 59, 61
Akyem, 49, 106, 121
Anlo, 31–33, 93, 94
Asante, 6, 13, 18, 20, 27, 28, 31, 35, 36, 39, 42, 43, 47, 49, 50, 56, 61, 65, 74, 89, 119
  kingdom of, 17, 27, 32, 35
  Region, 66, 67, 68, 88, 113
  wars, 22
Ashanti Farmers Association, 61
Banana, 22, 75, 77, 78, 80, 88, 123, 156
Banda country, 11
Basel Mission, 51, 52, 53
Bauxite, 113–115, 148
Beer, 46
Begho, 13, 23
Bono Mansu, 13
Brass, 46
British Cotton Growing Association, 42, 84
Bronze, 5
  Age, 7, 9, 21
Cape Coast, 49, 50, 52, 94, 119, 121, 169

Cape Coast Castle, 28
Carpentry, 53, 136
Cassava, 22, 30, 31, 38, 89
Castor oil, 75
Cattle, 13, 31, 91, 92, 157
  rearing, 15
Central districts, 22, 31, 92
Central Region, 39, 40, 78, 87, 119, 140
Christiansborg, 28, 31, 32, 86
Citrus, 77, 78, 87, 140
Cloth, 17, 18, 26, 31, 42, 49
Cocoa, 39, 44–46, 57–61, 64–67, 69, 71, 72, 75–77, 81, 96, 154–156, 160, 161, 164
  diseases, 65, 66, 77, 155
  exports, 60, 62, 64, 123
  industry, 59, 60, 61, 65
  Marketing Board, 76, 101, 126, 128, 145, 148, 156
  pool, 64
  price, 62, 64, 125, 128, 143, 146, 155, 156, 160
  production, 58, 125, 155
Coconut, 75, 77, 80, 82, 86, 87, 140
Cocoyams, 38, 88, 89
Communications, 105, 106, 116, 117, 121, 123
Construction, 158
Co-operative Societies, 60, 64, 65, 75, 79, 84, 88, 166
Coffee, 4, 45, 46, 71, 72, 75, 78, 88, 156
  price of, 156
Copper, 5, 9, 12, 46, 66
  bars, 16
Cote d'Ivoire, 11, 30, 49, 58, 125
Cotton, 17, 18, 22, 41, 43, 71, 72, 77, 78, 84–86, 137, 156
  development, 42, 43, 84, 85
  industry, 42, 43, 85
  goods, 123, 134
Cowries, 46
Crafts, 15, 33, 35, 52, 53, 137
Crude oil, cost of, 160

Currencies, 13, 14, 47
Dessication, 5, 7
Dagomba, 6
Development Plan, 121, 143, 146, 150, 151
Development Secretariat, 145
Diamond, 107, 110, 111, 156
  production, 111, 112, 158
  polishing, 145
  price of, 125, 126
Diversification, 74, 76, 81, 82, 156
Domestication, of animals, 1, 4, 5, 7
Domestic slavery, 14
Dye-wood, 12
Eastern districts, 39, 40
Eastern Region, 39, 40, 57, 59, 60, 65–67, 83, 88, 113, 119, 155
Economic Recovery Programme, 162

Education, technical, 146, 161
Elmina, 49, 52, 119
Elmina Castle, 11
English Royal African Company, 28, 35
Exchange economy, 5
Exports, 123, 124
Extractive industries, 15, 33, 34, 37, 52, 54, 135
Ewe, 6
Fante, 27, 28
Farming, 15, 21, 22, 34, 35, 39, 42, 59
Finance, 105, 127
Fire arms, 31, 35
Fishing, 15, 19, 34, 37, 92–96, 157
Food crop, 88, 89
Foreign exchange, 152, 155–157
Forestry, 15, 96, 157
  Department, 136
Ga, 6
Ghana Industrial Holding Corporation, 145, 153
Ginger, 156
Global 2000, 162
Gold Coast Farmers Association, 61
Gold, 9–14, 16, 18–21, 23, 26, 29, 32, 37, 39, 46, 54, 106, 156, 160, 168, 169

extraction, 16
export of, 12, 107, 123
mining, 9, 10, 15, 16, 34, 36
prices, 125, 126, 160
production, 10, 16, 27, 106, 107, 109, 158
smithing, 138
source of, 10, 11
trade, 10–12, 21, 22, 26, 27, 35
workings, 10
Gonja Development Corporation, 74
Guinea corn, 4, 30, 88
Gum copal, 46
Gun powder, 31, 35, 38, 46
Groundnut, 22, 38, 43, 46, 72, 74, 75, 77, 78, 82, 140, 153
Imports, 123, 124, 125, 126, 134, 138, 139
Indian corn, 30, 31, 38, 46
Indigenization, 153
Indigo, 13, 31
Industrial Development Corporation, 95, 143, 145–147
Industrialization, 84, 105, 121, 134, 135, 136, 141–148, 151–153, 155, 160, 162
  programme, 147, 148, 164
Industry, 15–17, 20, 33–35, 37, 38, 41, 42, 44, 45, 58, 62, 67, 82, 94, 156

Iron, 12, 14, 16, 19, 20, 46
  Age, 14, 22
  bars, 16, 33
  extraction of, 15
  goods, 20
  slag, 15
  smelting, 7, 15–17, 23, 33, 36
  workings, 9, 15, 16
Irrigation, 157
Ivory, 12, 29, 30, 32, 46
Kintampo, 13, 21, 50
Kola, 4, 13, 20, 50, 80, 123
Krepi, 33, 42, 49
Krobo, 22, 39, 40, 42, 56, 59
Kumasi, 31, 32, 47, 49, 52, 99, 113, 119, 120, 121, 139
Lead, 46

Livestock, 88, 91, 92, 157
Lower Volta, 31, 32, 42, 51, 93
Maize, 4, 22, 74, 78, 88, 89, 162
Mallaguetta pepper, 38, 46
Mande, 11, 23
Mandingo community, 11
Manganese, 113
    production of, 158
Manufacturing industries, 15, 33, 34, 37, 42, 43, 52, 53, 54, 134, 135–137, 139–141, 143–145, 147–149, 152–154
Masonry, 53
Mechanization, 74, 76, 81, 82, 156
Middle East, 1
Millet, 1, 4, 22, 74, 75, 78, 88
Minerals, production of, 116, 120, 123, 158
Mining, 15, 16, 20, 34, 105, 106, 158
    companies, 108, 109
Moshie, 6, 13
Multinational companies, 125, 144, 148, 161, 162
Murdock, Professor G. P., 1, 4
Native Authorities, 119, 120
Neolithic economy, 4
Neolithic period, 4, 5
Neolithic Revolution, 1, 4, 6, 7, 168
New Stone Age, 5, 22
New World, 25, 28, 30
Nigeria, 58, 81, 92, 99, 124, 125, 143, 167, 168
Ningo, 28, 31, 32, 49
Northern Ghana, 18, 39
Northern Region, 40, 42, 74, 75, 78, 84, 89, 91, 120
Northern traffic, 20, 30
Oil exploration, 158
Oil palm, 1, 4, 22, 30, 37, 38, 40, 41, 75, 80–82, 156
    industry, 38, 40, 41, 44, 81, 82
    origins of, 37
Palm kernels, 40, 41, 46, 53, 81, 82, 123, 139, 140
Palm products, 40, 41
    trade in, 40

Pawning, 14
Pepper, 12
Pineapples, 75, 156
Plantains, 22, 38
Pottery, 15, 17, 53, 136, 139
    fragments, 15
Railway, 120, 136
    Accra–Kumasi, 120
    Accra–Tema, 144
    Achiasi–Kotoku, 121
    Central Region, 120
    Sekondi–Kumasi, 120, 121
Rice, 1, 4, 22, 72, 75, 78, 88, 89, 91
Roads, 47, 49, 51, 52, 116, 117, 119–121
Rubber, 4, 38, 43–45, 80, 83, 84, 96
    export, 44, 123
    production, 83
    plantations, 44
    origins of, 43
Rum, 31, 35, 50

Salaga, 13, 21, 27, 32, 50, 51
Salt, 10, 17–19, 32
    manufacturing, 15, 19, 34
Sasakawa Programme, 162
Shea butter, 4, 156
    price of, 156, 160
Sheep, 13, 31, 50, 91, 92, 157
Silks, 46
Southern Ghana, 39
Southern traffic, 11, 20, 49
Spirits, 46
State Enterprises Secretariat, 145
State Farms Corporation, 79, 80, 82, 85
State Mining Corporation, 112
Sugar, 46, 145, 156
Sweet potatoes, 22
Takoradi, 99, 108, 113, 121, 137
Tarkwa, 52, 54, 55, 106, 110, 113, 121, 153, 168
Tea, 46
Tema, 121, 153
Textiles, 31, 53, 85, 137, 147, 153
Third World, 56, 60, 126, 162

Timber, 1, 29, 96–99, 105, 124, 137, 157, 160
  exploitation, 30, 97, 98
  export, 29, 97, 99, 123
Tobacco, 31, 35, 46, 49, 50, 78, 147
Togoland, 6, 55, 56, 78, 117, 168, 169
Trade, Atlantic, 12, 13, 36, 47
  in slaves, 25–36, 39, 40
  local, 46
  long-distance, 20, 21
  internal, 20
  international, 14, 29, 37, 46, 47, 49, 56, 64, 123, 125
  routes, 31, 32, 47, 49, 50, 51
Trading centres, 13, 14, 47, 49
Transportation, 5, 29, 32, 50–52, 85, 92, 97, 98
Trans-Saharan traffic, 11, 50
United Ghana Farmers Council, 79
Volta Region, 18, 26, 28, 32, 42, 66, 67, 78, 84, 85, 88, 117, 119, 120, 121, 137, 138

Volta River Project, 114, 115, 131, 143, 148
Wangara, 13
Wax, 12
Weaving, 15, 136–138
West African Cocoa Research Institute, 66
West African Oil Seeds Mission, 74
Western districts, 22, 31, 39
Western Region, 39, 57, 66, 78, 86–88, 113, 114, 110, 120
West Indian Company, 28
Wines, 46
Winneba, 49
Woodworks, 19
World war, First, 41, 45, 84, 113, 116, 117, 139
  Second, 66, 72, 74, 76, 82, 83, 86, 88, 89, 91, 95–97, 107–109, 111, 113, 119, 120, 125, 126, 134–140, 144
Yam, 4, 22, 38, 88, 89